Anonymous

Jubilee of the Strabane Presbyterian Church

historical sketch, sermons and addresses delivered at the fiftieth anniversary of its

organization, May 9-16, 1897.

Anonymous

Jubilee of the Strabane Presbyterian Church
historical sketch, sermons and addresses delivered at the fiftieth anniversary of its organization, May 9-16, 1897.

ISBN/EAN: 9783337264550

Printed in Europe, USA, Canada, Australia, Japan

Cover: Foto ©Lupo / pixelio.de

More available books at **www.hansebooks.com**

South-East View.

..Jubilee..

.... OF THE ....

Strabane
Presbyterian Church

HISTORICAL SKETCH,
SERMONS AND ADDRESSES

DELIVERED AT THE

FIFTIETH ANNIVERSARY

OF ITS ORGANIZATION

May 9-16, 1897.

MACPHERSON & DROPE,
PRINTERS,
CORNER OF JAMES AND REBECCA STREETS,
HAMILTON, CANADA.

PREFACE.

THIS little volume is not prepared for the general public, but for a comparatively small circle of readers. Neither is it to be put in the book market for sale, but is presented to the members and friends of the pastoral charge of Strabane and Kilbride, who have manifested an interest in the celebration of the fiftieth anniversary to the extent of contributing at least one dollar as a Jubilee offering.

The historical portion is in the form of a simple narrative, embracing the more important events which have transpired during the last half century within the little circle of our church home. While the writer has aimed at being faithful and impartial in the statement of facts which were regarded as necessary in a sketch of this kind, he has purposely omitted everything which, in the judgment of the session, would be better forgotten. Fuller information would have been given on some points if it could have been procured, and it is quite probable that incidents and personal references worthy of record have been inadvertently passed over, for which we ask in advance the pardon of our readers.

The Session would respectfully dedicate this volume to the three "mothers in Israel," viz: Mrs. James Nicol, Mrs. James Reid and Mrs. Nathaniel Gregg, who sat at the communion table fifty years ago, and who in the providence of God are still with us in the flesh, and would pray, that as the links which unite us with the past are being severed one by one, all into whose hands this book may come, may be united by faith with Jesus and made partakers of the reward which He has promised to those who love and serve Him.

CONTENTS.

HISTORICAL SKETCH BY REV. D. G. CAMERON.

CHAP. I   ..   EARLY SETTLEMENT TO ORGANIZATION.

CHAP. II   ..   ORGANIZATION AND INSTALLMENT OF FIRST PASTOR.

CHAP. III   ..   PASTORATE OF REV. ALEXANDER McLEAN AT CUMMINSVILLE AND NAIRN CHURCH.

CHAP. IV   ..   PASTORATE OF REV. ALEXANDER McLEAN AT NAIRN CHURCH.

CHAP. V   ..   ..   PASTORATE OF REV. JOHN L. ROBERTSON.

CHAP. VI   ..   PASTORATES OF REVS. W. H. SIMPSON AND J. CAMPBELL, AT KILBRIDE.

CHAP. VII   ..   PASTORATE OF REV. J. W. CATHCART.

CHAP. VIII   PASTORATE OF REV. D. G. CAMERON.

CHAP. IX   ..   ..   THE JUBILEE.

THREE SERMONS
BY
THE REV. THOS. WARDROPE, D. D.
THE REV. JOHN YOUNG, M. A.
THE REV. W. A. McKAY, D. D.

CHAPTER I.

EARLY SETTLEMENT TO ORGANIZATION.

A PERSON who has never visited Strabane, in order to locate it will require to glance at a map of Ontario. Wentworth county, which doubles around Burlington Bay, at the western extremity of Lake Ontario, is easily found. Look at the three northern townships: Beverley, square and compact; East Flamboro, somewhat narrower; and West Flamboro between the two, triangular in shape with the apex pointing northward. The Grand Trunk railway runs westward from the City of Hamilton, near the southern boundary of West Flamboro. Five miles west of the city is the town of Dundas; from which, extending northward through the centre of the township is the Brock Road, which continues its course through Guelph and Fergus as far north as the Georgian Bay. This road was opened about the year 1825.

A large tract of land in this vicinity had been granted by the crown to the heirs of the brave general who fell in the defense of his country at Queenston Heights in 1812. From these heirs, or their agents, the first settlers purchased their farms. The road was originally intended to open up a highway to these lands, hence it was called the Brock Road.

Dundas, in those early days, was the head of navigation for Lake Ontario, and from this point the Brock Road was the highway to the settlements lying to the north. The traffic on this road became very great as the country was opened up, and the demand for the accommodation of travellers at intervals on their journey was amply supplied. The taverns, as they were called, were numerous, although for comfort they may not have been all that a weary traveller could desire. Whatever might be said of board and bedding, the universal testimony is that there was always plenty to drink.

With the exception of the tavern keepers along the way who had made small clearings around their shanties, this section was unbroken forest until the year 1835. There appeared to be a preference for the land lying farther north. At that time the road was in a very primitive condition, the smaller trees and brushwood only being removed, the trail was somewhat out of line, often swerving from its course to avoid the large pines which mingled their branches overhead.

Over this road, lonely and difficult to travel, there passed, at certain seasons, an almost continuous procession of settlers with their families and effects in waggons drawn by oxen. When asked

THE LATE THOS. WARDROPE.

where they intended to locate they invariably answered, "In the Queen's bush," which was understood to designate the unsurveyed district beyond Guelph.

At a point on the Brock road where it is intersected by the 8th concession of West Flamboro, ten miles north of Dundas and sixteen miles south of Guelph, is the little village of Strabane. A mile and a half further north is a village considerably larger, named Freelton. It is to the smaller hamlet, however, that attention is now directed as the centre of Presbyterianism in this locality.

In the spring of 1835 a few families took up homesteads in this vicinity. They were not all of one creed or nationality, but that did not prevent them from building a school house which was intended to serve the double purpose of school and church, where they might have the children educated, and where children and parents of whatever phase of Christian faith might unite in the worship of God. The first school house, a plain frame building, was erected where the present school now stands, in the autumn of 1835. The neighborhood was visited from time to time by ministers and missionaries of various denominations, all of whom were made welcome and their services well attended.

Among those who settled on the 9th concession of West Flamboro' in 1840 was Mr. Thomas Wardrope, who with his family had come from

Scotland in 1834. Mr. Wardrope was a licentiate of the Church of Scotland and was for many years parish schoolmaster at Lady Kirk, in Berwickshire. The time intervening between 1834 and 1840 he spent partly in the Township of Guelph and partly in Puslinch, in which places he had frequently preached. The news soon spread that Mr. Wardrope was a minister. The Presbyterians were specially interested in this, and upon inquiry found that he had been educated for the ministry of the Presbyterian Church, but that he had not been ordained. The matter of ordination was, however, regarded as a very secondary consideration, which might be attended to later on. Upon invitation of the people, Mr. Wardrope conducted weekly service in the school and visited the various families in the neighborhood. The fact of having a minister of their own denomination living among them was regarded with favor by the Presbyterians and acknowledged by all as giving special visibility to that denomination.

Regular Sabbath services were now held, Mr. Wardrope gracefully giving way to other ministers when they came and preaching himself on the intervening Sabbaths.

The necessity for a church building soon became apparent, and the question of ways and means was frequently discussed. The people were poor and had no prospect of help beyond themselves. The question as to where the church should be built was soon decided when John Fraser offered to give, free of charge, a suitable lot next to the school property upon which to erect a Presbyterian church ; the only condition attached being that the building should be named Nairn Church, in honor of his Highland home across the sea. This proposal was heartily accepted by the promoters of the enterprise, whereupon Mr. Fraser made the additional offer that if the others would provide the logs he would without charge saw the lumber necessary for the building at his mill near by. All were willing to accept such a generous proposal and seemed eager to get to work to do their full share in providing the lumber. But Mr. Wardrope reminded them that other material would be necessary besides lumber and that while the bulk of the labour could be performed by making "bees" they would require the help of a skilled workman to make the windows, door and seats. This point was soon settled when John Sanderson, " frae Aberdeen awa," a carpenter by trade, volunteered as his share to mark out the frame, to make the doors and windows and also to make a pulpit; while Walter McFarlane, who in his young days had been a ship carpenter, volunteered to lay the floor and assist in the inside finishing. Nathaniel Gregg from the Emerald Isle, was a weaver, but as carpets were not mentioned in the estimates there seemed no call for his handiwork. Knowing, however, that nails, glass and other hardware must be bought, he drew up a subscription list, heading it with a handsome sum and secured from others the promise of sufficient for the purpose.

Already there arose in the mental vision a view of Nairn Church in all its completeness and beauty, crowning the rising knoll on the west side of the Brock Road, with groups of happy people greeting one another on a bright Sabbath morning as they went up to the house of the Lord. Our fathers and mothers were hopeful in their prospects and doubtless offered many a fervent prayer that they and their dear children might in Nairn Church receive precious instruction and guidance in life's dangerous journey.

But the pines from which the church was to be built were still standing in the forest. During the winter of 1843 the logs were brought to Mr. Fraser's mill. Among those who assisted in this work besides those already named were Alexander Stewart, William Stephenson, James McCuen, James Reid, John Reid, John Duffis, James Wardrope, John Ferrier, Andrew Waddell, and Alex. Findlay.

While the work of providing logs was in progress a sad event took place. Andrew Waddell while engaged in loading a heavy log required some help. His wife taking in the situation at a glance, came to his assistance. Their only child, about a year and a half old, being with her was left standing at what was considered a safe distance. Through some mishap the log rolled from the skid in the direction of the child and before any effort could be put forth he was crushed to death before their eyes. It was a sore trial to the parents and for the time cast a gloom over the entire neighborhood.

As soon as the lumber was ready a "bee" was made to frame and erect the church. Another was made to put on the roof. Even Presbyterian zeal, it must be admitted, sometimes flags, and so it appears that our fathers concluded that the kirk might "bide a wee." Thus it stood through the fall and winter and well on through the following summer with only the frame and roof. It might have stood longer in that condition had it not been that a stranger passing through taunted John Sanderson with the unsightly appearance of the church, saying "You Presbyterians began to build and were not able to finish." Mr. Sanderson set a good example by taking the taunt in the right spirit and turning it to good account. He went to work at the church the following day assisted by his son James (who is still with us). Day after day he wrought saying that even if no one else would put a hand to it he would work on till it would be finished. Others influenced by his decision came to his assistance. Walter McFarlane, John Reid and James Wardrope laid the floor, John Fraser and Nathanial Gregg succeeded in raising $30 which they gave to Mr. Sanderson requesting him to go on and complete the job. The work of church building for the time being was now at an end. There was no formal dedication. Mr. Wardrope continued his work, occasionally exchanging with Mr. Stark of Dundas or Mr. Christie of Flamboro, in order that those desiring to have their children baptized might do so more conveniently.

Thus the work went quietly on until June, 1847. Although the fact was known to the Presbytery that there was a congregation here, with a church building and regular services, no effort was put forth to have it formally organized or taken under presbyterial oversight. One reason for this may have been that what is known as the Disruption, which took place in Scotland in 1843 was succeeded by a similar movement in Canada during the following year, although with much less expression of feeling. Those ministers and congregations in western Canada who sympathized with the Free Church movement were organized into a Free Church Synod, known as the Presbyterian Church of Canada. The organization took place in Kingston in June, 1844. Rev. M. Y. Stark, of Dundas, was the first moderator. Among the Presbyteries organized under this Synod was the Presbytery of Hamilton, of which Rev. Geo. Smellie, of Fergus, was Moderator, and Rev. Mr. Stark was Clerk.

Mr. Wardrope was much beloved by his people who were now beginning to consider it their duty to have his relation to them take a more permanent form. They drew up and signed a petition (which was virtually a call) and presented it by a deputation to the Presbytery of Hamilton, asking that court to ordain Mr. Wardrope and install him as their pastor. The action taken on this petition is set forth in the official document of which the following is a copy:

" At a meeting of the Presbytery of Hamilton in connection with the Presbyterian Church of Canada, held at Hamilton on the fourteenth day of January, one thousand eight hundred and forty-seven, an application from the congregation in the eighth concession of Flamboro West to have a call moderated in to Mr. Thomas Wardrope, senior, preacher of the gospel, to be their minister, was given in and read, and a deputation from the congregation was heard in support of it. Mr. Wardrope being present was interrogated as to his own views in the matter and stated that he put himself entirely at the disposal of the Presbytery to do as they thought best for the interests of the Redeemer's kingdom in that corner of the vineyard.

The Presbytery after mature deliberation agreed to refer the case to the Synod for advice, feeling that at Mr. Wardrope's advanced age he could not be expected fully to discharge the duties of a settled pastor to such a congregation, and doubtful on these grounds as well as his own hesitation about accepting the charge, the propriety of his being ordained pastor of the congregation.

The Presbytery, however, in the meantime appointed Mr. Stark, Mr. Bayne and Mr. Meldrum, along with Mr. Smellie, the Moderator of Presbytery, a committee to visit the congregation to make arrangements for preaching there, taking steps to organize the congregation, to ordain elders and dispense the sacrament of the Lord's Supper, at a period not later than the end of March ensuing.

Accordingly, on Friday the nineteenth day of March, as by appointment previously made, and after notice duly given, Mr. Stark preached to the congregation, served the edict for the ordination of the persons elected to the office of the eldership, and after divine service did, along with the Rev. George Smellie and Rev. William Meldrum, examine Mr. John Sanderson, Mr. Walter McFarlane, Mr. James Nicol and Mr. James Brown, and finding them in so far as they could judge, suitably qualified, resolved to proceed on the following day, as instructed, to ordain them to the office of the eldership, in the event of no valid reason being shown why this should not be done.

On the following day accordingly, the Rev. George Smellie having conducted divine service, and none having compeered to object, did by prayer set apart the above said persons as elders of the congregation and addressed them solemnly

JOHN SANDERSON.

WALTER McFARLANE.

JAMES NICOL.

The First Elders of Nairn Church.

and earnestly in regard to their duties. Mr. Stark afterwards addressed the congregation. Whereupon the session was constituted by Mr. Smellie, and according to intimation applicants for admission to the Lord's Table were examined and such as were found qualified received tokens.

The next day being Sabbath, Mr. Smellie by appointment preached and presided at the dispensation of the Lord's Supper and Mr. Stark assisted. Fifty-five communicants sat down at the table and many it is hoped experienced it to be a feast of good things.

At a subsequent meeting of the Presbytery of Hamilton, held at Hamilton on the twelfth day of May following, the report of the above proceedings was heard and the diligence of the committee approved.

A letter from Mr. Wardrope to the Clerk stating that after mature and prayerful deliberation he thought it better to decline the desire of the congregation that he should be ordained as their pastor, owing to his advanced age and increasing infirmities, was given in and read. Whereupon it was moved and agreed to that the Presbytery having heard Mr. Wardrope's letter, express their approbation of the excellent spirit which it breathes, agree to withdraw their proposed application to the Synod for advice in his case and to concur in the wish he expresses to labor as heretofore as God may enable him, without being ordained to the office of the ministry and connected with the congregation of West Flamboro as their regular minister, and that therefore this congregation as now organized be placed under the general superintendence of the Rev. M. Y. Stark, the Rev. Geo. Smellie, the Rev. Wm. Meldrum and such other minister as may be appointed to the congregation at Guelph. The elders to communicate with Mr. Stark or other of the above named members of Presbytery in regard to dispensation of ordinances, cases of discipline or matters in which they may require advice or direction."

The above statement containing a narrative of the circumstances connected with the organization and recognition by the Presbytery of Hamilton of the congregation in the eighth concession of West Flamboro was drawn up and is attested by

M. Y. STARK,
Clerk of the Presbytery of Hamilton.

May 12th, 1847.

LIST OF PERSONS PRESENT AT THE FIRST COMMUNION.

Alexander Reid
Mrs. Alexander Reid
James Reid
Mrs. James Reid
William Stephenson
Mrs. Wm. Stephenson
Nathaniel Gregg
Mrs. Nathaniel Gregg
James Nicol
Mrs. James Nicol
Hugh Thomson
Mrs. Hugh Thomson
Duncan McFarlane
Mrs. Duncan McFarlane
Mrs. Edington and
   three daughters
Mrs. Logan
John Sanderson, sr.
Mrs. John Sanderson
Miss Sanderson
James Brown
Mrs. James Brown
Walter McFarlane
Mrs Walter McFarlane
William Stewart
John Waddell
Mrs. John Waddell

William Connell
Mrs. William Connell
William Johnstone
John Duffis
Mrs. John Duffis
John Purvis
Mrs. John Purvis
Mrs. Waddell
Walter Robertson
Mrs. Walter Robertson
William Bell
Thomas Wardrope, sr.
Mrs. Thomas Wardrope
James Wardrope
George Watson
William Paton
Alexander Findlay
Mrs. Alex. Findlay
Andrew Miller
James Gilmour
Mrs. James Gilmour
John Sanderson, jr.
Catherine Brennan
Alexander Stewart
Margaret Forrest
Mrs. John Gilmour

Mr. Wardrope, who was at this time 67 years of age, continued his work as formerly. His eldest son, Thomas, had completed his studies for the ministry. David and George, two younger sons, were at college with the ministry in view. Here we must leave him for the present in his home on the 9th concession in order to trace the movements of the minister who in the providence of God was to succeed to the position of first settled pastor of Nairn Church.

CHAPTER II.

FROM THE ORGANIZATION TO THE INDUCTION OF
REV. ALEXANDER McLEAN.

ALEXANDER McLEAN was descended from the McLeans of Duart, in the island of Mull, Scotland. His immediate forefathers removed to Paisley, where for some years they resided. Here, the glowing accounts of America attracted public attention, and the McLeans were among those in that locality who decided to emigrate. Accordingly, a company of some fifty families sailed for the new world, accompanied by a Presbyterian minister in the person of Rev. John Witherspoon, who afterwards became famous in American history as a signer of the Declaration of Independence, and who was widely known in his day, not only as a divine but also as an author and statesman, and who being on the most intimate terms with George Washington, rendered valuable assistance in framing the Constitution of the United States, on which occasion the Presbyterian system of church government was largely in evidence as a model.

The colony from Paisley settled in Saratoga County, N. Y. Mr. McLean's father at one time owned the land on which has since grown up the city of Saratoga Springs. Prior to the settlement of this colony, the relation between Britain and New England had become somewhat strained and the spirit of revolution spread so that it seemed impossible for anyone to remain neutral. The Scottish settlers of Saratoga, although united in religion and many of them by kindred ties, found it necessary in order to be true to their convictions, to take opposite sides. While their pastor, as already stated, threw his energies into the foremost ranks of the revolutionists, several of his former parishioners remained unshaken in their loyalty to the King and to British connection. The war of Independence which broke out in 1775 and lasted till 1782, compelled those who would not take up arms against Britain to seek safety in flight, thus forfeiting their beautiful homesteads with all the results of years of industry and toil.

Among the many who made their way northward to the Canadian frontier in batteaux via Lakes George and Champlain, were the parents of the subject of this sketch. As a reward for their loyalty and compensation for their losses, they received, with many other United Empire Loyalists, a grant of 200 acres on the north bank of the St. Lawrence, near where the town of Brockville now stands. It was in their new home on British soil that Alexander was born in the year 1815.

He received such early education as could be afforded by the schools of those times. He soon learned to read the Bible, which was the principal book in use, and became acquainted with its teachings. Early in life he was led to profess his faith in Christ and choose the Lord as the guide of his youth, resolving to follow whithersoever His Providence directed. He soon became possessed of an ardent desire to become a preacher of the Gospel. Strange to say, his father was averse to such a course and endeavored to turn his son's mind in the direction of a business career, offering him inducements to remain where the land they had taken was rapidly increasing in value. Young McLean's heart, however, was so set upon becoming a minister that even his father's refusal to defray the expense of a college education did not turn him from his purposes. His loyalty to what he regarded as the will of the King of Heaven was no less intense than that of his father regarding the will of the King of England. Leaving behind parents, friends, home and inducements to worldly advancement, he entered upon a course of study at a grammar school at Potsdam, Vermont, where he received his preparatory education. How he procured the necessary means we are unable to state, but a youth with his ambition and high aim usually succeeds in overcoming even financial difficulties in an honorable way, by teaching or other honorable employment.

We next find him in Edinburgh, Scotland, where he received his University and Theological training, studying Divinity under the celebrated Dr. Chalmers. On the completion of his studies he was licensed to preach the Gospel. Considerable interest was centered upon him at that time in church circles, on account of the fact that he was the first Canadian-born student which Edinburgh had trained for the Gospel ministry.

It was in the autumn of 1842 that he returned to Canada and placed himself under the care of the Presbytery of Kingston. In February, 1843, he was ordained and inducted as the first pastor of Picton, in Prince Edward County. In the following year he cast in his lot with those who took part in the Disruption movement, already referred to, and was one of the first members of the Free Church Synod. His labours in Picton were only well commenced when he was compelled to spend a season in Georgia for the benefit of his health. He soon returned to his congregation quite restored and was shortly afterwards married to Miss Elizabeth Miller, a daughter of one of the most enterprising pioneers of that place.

In 1846 he received and accepted a call to Wellington Square and Waterdown in the Presbytery of Hamilton. Although not included in the name of the pastoral charge, Cumminsville, a stirring little village about eight miles north of Waterdown, where were a few Presbyterian families, was recognized as a mission station under Mr. McLean's oversight. Here he preached once a month at first but soon gave a week day service as well, which brought him to the village once a fortnight. The cause prospered under his ministry. Shortly it was found that Cumminsville gained in numbers and strength sufficient to enable them to offer to pay one-third of the minister's salary and claim a corresponding share of his services. The services were held wherever the most suitable quarters could be secured—a tavern kitchen, a tannery and a log school house serving their turn.

Suitable property for a church and burying ground was secured on the high ground opposite the village. The church was built in 1849. On February 9th, 1850, the first communion was observed—the elders from the other congregations officiating—when thirty-one persons sat at the table of the Lord. In February, 1852, two elders were elected and ordained, viz., William Carr and David Agnew. Subsequently these with William Wilson, of Waterdown, officiated at the communions held in Cumminsville, which were once a year.

In the autumn of 1854, the attention of Presbytery having been directed to the possibility of a better arrangement of the mission stations in this locality, a deputation was appointed to consult with the parties interested.

Upon hearing the report of this deputation, at a meeting of Presbytery held on January 9th, 1855, Cumminsville was separated from Wellington Square and Waterdown and united with Nairn

Church, to form a pastoral charge, in which there was to be but one session composed of the elders within the bounds.

The people of Cumminsville being desirous of retaining the services of their minister and the people of Nairn Church being equally willing to accept him as their pastor, and Mr. McLean consenting to such arrangement, the Presbytery resolved to induct him as pastor of the united charge, concerning which event we make the following quotation from the private diary of Mr. McLean:

" May 23rd, 1855—Was inducted at Cumminsville. Mr. McAuley of Nassagaweya preached, Mr. Stark put the questions and addressed the minister, and Mr. Young of Guelph, the people. It was a solemn scene, many attending. Give grace, guidance and success in the field, O Lord. Give me souls for Jesus' crown.

June 8th, 1855—Removed to Cumminsville. O may each move be nearer Heaven and Christ."

CHAPTER III.

MR. McLEAN'S PASTORATE AT CUMMINSVILLE AND NAIRN CHURCH.

LESS than a mile west of Cumminsville a rival village had, within a few years, sprung into existence, named Kilbride, at which place the minister took up his residence in a rented house. The church which had been erected in 1849, a small frame structure 24 x 36 feet, was not large enough to accommodate the growing congregation. As Kilbride was regarded more central, a site was procured there on which to erect a church. The new building, which is still in a good state of preservation and likely to serve the congregation for many years to come, was dedicated to the worship of God in the autumn of 1856. A manse was required but the congregation did not feel able to build one so soon; consequently Mr. McLean bought a piece of land adjoining the church property on which he erected a large brick cottage, assuming all financial responsibility, and thus had, for a time at least, the satisfaction which few ministers enjoy, of living in a house planned according to his own ideal. Kilbride is situated in the Township of Nelson, County of Halton, and is, according to the map, about six miles east of Strabane, but on account of the hills those who frequently travel the road reckon on nearly seven miles.

In pastoral charges consisting of two congregations the place in which the minister resides and in which he preaches in the forenoon is usually regarded as the more important. Kilbride enjoyed this distinction and appears to have been at that time the more aggressive of the two, although in point of numbers they were about the same.

We have already learned that, prior to the union, two elders had been ordained at Cumminsville and four at Strabane. In the latter place Mr. Brown died soon after while Messrs. Carr and Agnew had either died or removed from the bounds, as their names do not again appear on the records. Mr. William Wilson (the grandfather of Rev. W. A. Wilson of Central India), was an elder before Cumminsville was organized. He, together with Messrs. Sanderson, McFarlane and Nicol of Strabane, formed the Session of the united charge.

Shortly after Mr. McLean's induction the members were asked to elect six additional elders —three from each congregation. On December 29th, 1856, the Session met for the purpose of counting the votes, with the result that the following were declared elected, viz.: for Nairn Church, John Coleman, James Robertson and James Wardrope; for Kilbride, Francis Small, sr., Archibald Campbell and John Agnew. All declined with the exception of James Wardrope who was duly ordained on May 21st, 1857, and his name added to the roll of Session.

At a weekday service held in Kilbride church on May 13th, 1858, the congregation was called upon to elect three elders, which was done by open vote, resulting in Messrs. Small, Campbell and Agnew being again the unanimous choice of the people. Mr. Small and Mr. Agnew accepted the office, and were ordained on October 23rd, 1858. Upon the same occasion Thomas Elliott, George Agnew, John Duffes, William Molineaux and Andrew Wilson were elected deacons: the last three accepted the office and were duly ordained. On the 2nd Sabbath of April, 1861, James Sanderson was ordained to the eldership in Nairn Church. The elders now numbered eight—three at Kilbride and five at Strabane. The work was advancing, the membership was increased at every communion and the Sabbath services were well attended.

At this point, just when the cause was being well established, we have to record an event which cannot be viewed but with regret. By an action of Presbytery these two struggling congregations, which by their united effort could support a pastor at a minimum salary, were separated and left to stand alone. Let not the reader conclude, however, that this arrangement was forced upon the people by the Presbytery. An unfortunate misunderstanding seems to have arisen between the pastor and a large section of the Kilbride congregation, concerning the particulars of which the writer has no information and into which he has no desire to inquire. A reference to the fact, however, is deemed necessary in order to explain such an unseemly separation. At a large meeting held in Nairn Chnrch, called for the purpose of discussing the situation, a resolution was passed, almost unanimously, requesting the Presbytery to erect Nairn Church into a separate self-sustaining charge under Mr. McLean's pastorate. Upon this petition the Presbytery took action as already stated, granting the prayer of the petition, and declaring Kilbride charge vacant on August 4th, 1861. As there was no manse or suitable house in Strabane, the congregation rented a house in Freelton, into which the minister immediately moved.

CHAPTER IV.

MR. McLEAN'S PASTORATE AT NAIRN CHURCH.

THE experience through which their pastor had just passed caused the people of Strabane to rally around him with assurances of sympathy and loyalty. The salary which they promised was not large but their personal gifts were numerous and as Mr. McLean had no children to provide for, he could get along nicely with what the people felt able to contribute.

The methods adopted in the management of congregational affairs in those days seem somewhat quaint to us of the present, as our methods also may appear to those who review our records fifty years hence. The size of the committees appear to be not in proper proportion to the size of the congregation. For example, in the year 1862 there were probably fifty or sixty families and about ninety communicants. For financial purposes the congregation was divided into fourteen districts. The Board of Management consisted of the pastor and the five elders already named, together with Messrs. Gregg, Elliott, Calder, Dunlop, Robertson, Findlay, Watt, McDougall, Moore, Fulton, Murray and Fletcher, eighteen in all. At the annual meeting it was "unanimously agreed that the following be elected to aid the managers," viz: Margaret Watson, Ellen Findlay, Margaret Campbell, Annie Stewart, Janet Robertson, Catherine Addison, Hannah Murray, Isabella Murray, Sarah Murray, Elizabeth Addison, Margaret Peebles, Mrs. McNeill, Martha Wilson, Thomas Murray, Matilda Peebles, Thomas Fletcher, and Elspeth Smith.

This enormous committee presented its report to the annual meeting of the congregation, of which complaint is recorded as to the smallness of the attendance. The money collected that year for pastor's salary was $270.65, ordinary and special collections $97.92.

In order to secure a better attendance at the annual meetings the pastor on one occasion delivered a lecture at the meeting on "Canadian Statistics," and upon another occasion on "The wanderings of the Children of Israel."

The earliest record of money raised for missionary purposes was made in 1863, when the congregation gave to Foreign Missions $2.25, Red River Mission $7, Widows' Fund $3, Home Missions $4.75, and French Canadian Missions $4, total $18.

For several years Mr. Gregg had been treasurer and continued to fill that office during the remainder of his life to the entire satisfaction of the congregation.

Mr. Wardrope by this time had become enfeebled by old age but still manifested a deep interest in the advancement of the cause which was so dear to him. The people regarded him with all the veneration and love due to a retired pastor still among them. On the 3rd of October, 1864, at the advanced age of 84 years, he entered upon his rest and reward. A plain marble slab a few yards from the south-east corner of the present church building marks the spot where his remains await the resurrection of the just.

Mr. Fraser died suddenly shortly after the church was built, and before trustees had been appointed, to whom he could convey the property, consequently there was unavoidable delay in securing a deed of the original site.

In 1866 there was an election of elders. Nine were nominated, viz., Thomas Bain, Duncan Murray, James Harper, N. Gregg, J. McDougall, A. Findlay, R. Lothian, R. Mackie and James Muir. The first four named were elected, but Duncan Murray alone accepted. He was ordained on the 14th of October.

About this time the propriety of building a manse was discussed at congregational meetings and two offers for land near the church on which to erect the building were under consideration. There was considerable diversity of opinion as to the price asked, and the suitability of the respective sites.

Mr. Sabin Bronson owned seven acres near the corner, on the 8th concession, on which he had a saw mill and dwelling house. Having met with the misfortune of losing his mill by fire he resolved to sell out his property and try his fortune elsewhere. As a result of two special meetings, held in February, 1867, between which a subscription list was hurriedly circulated, a bargain was made by which Mr. Bronson sold his property to the congregation for the sum of $600. Thomas Bain, James Sanderson and Duncan Murray were appointed Trustees for the manse property.

The loss which the congregation sustained by the removal of Mr. and Mrs. Bronson who had for several years led in the service of praise, was to a certain extent offset by the satisfaction of having secured at a moderate price such a large and convenient glebe.

The manse, a fairly good frame house, quite roomy and well sheltered by trees, was very much to the minister's liking. Although the stable was poor and the greater part of the land in a rough condition, marred by the ruins of the mill and dotted by large pine stumps and deserted and dilapidated shanties of the workmen, yet near the house was a young orchard of almost one hundred fruit trees which added to both the appearance and value. Soon after the purchase Mr. McLean took up his residence in "The Manse," which was his home during the remaining ten years of his mortal life.

The manifestations of spirituality and growth in grace among the members of the church, as far as could be judged by the Session, were of an encouraging character. In 1866, in its answers to the Synod's questions on the state of religion, the Session refers to the growing interest in the preaching of the Word. In the Sabbath School and in the home the pastor observes a "drawing of the young to Jesus," and sees among them "several marked manifestations of early grace." In stating to what extent the cause is injured by intemperance, the Session replies that it is "limited to the few families where the dram prevails—there every evil work is found." "Through the efforts of a temperance organization in the place, numbering in all about 150 members, the evil is greatly abated."

May, 1869, "The Session records its sense of the Lord's kindness towards the congregation in sparing so long the late beloved and esteemed Christian patriarch and elder of this church, Mr. John Sanderson, who fell asleep in Jesus on April 1st of this year and prays that a double portion of the Spirit may abide upon those who remain."

In 1867 the number on the communion roll was 146, and continued to increase until 1876, when after a careful revision, it numbered 170.

Progress marked the church finances also. The report of 1875 states that the amount received for stipend was $580.40, missions $96.30, ordinary collections $110.42. The Session and congregation joined heartily in the union of the various Presbyterian bodies in Canada which was consummated in Montreal in June, 1875.

The original church building, although small, proved large enough for a few years. When more room was required a contract for enlargement was given to Mr. Thomas Gray, who by the addition of two projections or wings, a new roof and some inside renovation, added much to its appearance and comfort.

Time, however, had left its marks on the edifice, so that even the wings were beginning to droop. A new church had been proposed, but the undertaking seemed so formidable, and the matter of procuring a site presented so many difficulties that progress in this direction was slow.

The necessity for horse sheds was advocated and over $100 raised for the purpose, but this also had to be held in abeyance until the title of the site on which the church stood as well as sufficient additional land adjoining should be secured, in order, if possible, to have a square with frontage on the Brock Road, sufficiently large for all requirements.

Thos. Bain was appointed by the congregation to negotiate in the purchase of this land while Richard Lothian, Jas. Muir and J. B. P. Robertson were appointed trustees. Mrs. Fraser, by letters of administration, was now in a position to transact business regarding the estate.

On February 7th, 1877, she gave to the trustees a deed which conveyed to the congregation the lot on which the church stood, out of deference to the promise made by her deceased husband, John Fraser. Also, in addition to this, as a gift from herself, the lot occupied as a burying ground. These two parcels contained 2 roods, 38 perches, or about three-quarters of an acre. On the same day she sold to the congregation one acre adjoining the church lot for the sum of $400. About a year after, the congregation purchased from Mrs. Fraser an additional quarter of an acre for the sum of $50. These gifts and purchases made up a desirable property containing two acres, more or less, compact in shape and beautiful for situation.

While this business was being transacted by the congregation, the pastor was becoming more feeble in health, the people remarked how grey he was getting and noticed that he was not able to attend night meetings, but none seemed to suspect that the end of his journey was so near. We present to the reader an engraving from a photograph taken about six years before his death, which is said to be a true likeness. His most striking characteristics seem to have been the kindliness of his disposition manifested in a special manner in his attitude towards the children, of whom he was passionately fond, and the simplicity of his life among his brethren. An illustration of the latter might be given. On one occasion he spent the night at the manse of a brother minister who had half a dozen lively children with whom he was accustomed to play. The children, who followed one another in close succession on the family register, were accustomed to follow the same order in climbing to their father's shoulder, and, holding his hands, turn a somersault, alighting on their feet or otherwise on the carpet. Mr. McLean looked on with silence and manifest anxiety at the game in which he saw only danger to the little ones, and although he uttered no remark at the time, when he came to conduct family worship, he fervently thanked God that none of the children had sustained bodily injury by the experience through which they had just passed.

During the winter of 1877 he labored with difficulty to overtake his work, keeping at his post of duty as long as he was able. After being but one Sabbath out of the pulpit his strength rapidly gave way and on March 3rd, 1877, he was called to rest from his labours.

In compliance with his own request, his remains were interred close to the west end of the church directly behind the pulpit in which he had faithfully proclaimed the Gospel message for twenty-two years. A plain headstone now marks the spot, on which is inscribed :

IN MEMORY OF

REV. ALEXANDER McLEAN

Died March 3rd, 1877,

AGED 62 YEARS.

*I have preached righteousness, I have not refrained my lips,
O Lord, thou knowest.*

THE LATE REV. A McLEAN.

Shortly after his death a meeting of Session was held, with Rev. S. W. Fisher as moderator *pro tem*, at which the following resolution was adopted :

"The Session would desire to place upon record their deep sense of the loss they have sustained as a congregation in the removal by death of their beloved pastor, the Rev. Alexander McLean, who for the past twenty-two years has labored among them so faithfully amidst all the discouragements of a new settlement. They would express their high estimation of his many estimable qualities as a Christian gentleman, genial, happy and cheerful in all his intercourse with his flock, and withal possessed of a charming simplicity ; of his faithfulness as a pastor, especially in visiting the sick ; of his substantial abilities as a minister of the glorious gospel of Jesus Christ, of which it was his great joy to tell sinners; of the lively interest he ever took in the young under his care, as well as the deep concern he ever manifested in the spiritual welfare and prosperity of the whole congregation. They would also express their deep sympathy with the bereaved widow in the irreparable loss she has thereby sustained, and pray that " the peace of God which passeth all understanding may keep her heart and mind through Christ Jesus."

CHAPTER V.

PASTORATE OF REV. J. L. ROBERTSON.

WHEN the usual arrangements were made for the supply of the pulpit, and an opportunity given to make choice of a minister to succeed Mr. McLean, the congregation acted with commendable promptness. At a meeting called for the purpose on August 15th, 1877, a unanimous call was extended to the Rev. John L. Robertson, M. A., accompanied by a guarantee of $700 salary and a free manse. The call was sustained and accepted, and the induction took place on the 11th of September.

Mr. Robertson was born of Scottish parentage, on Canadian soil, near the historic battle ground of Queenston Heights. His early education was received in St. Catharines Grammar School, and the Normal School, Toronto. After teaching for a short time in Canada he went to the United States, where he studied for the ministry at Westminster College, under the direction of the United Presbyterian Church. He was licensed to preach in 1867, and was ordained by the Presbytery of Stamford as pastor of the U. P. Church, Walton, Ont., in September of the same year. After about a year

REV. JOHN L. ROBERTSON, M. A.

and a half he returned to Pennsylvania, **where he was** in a settled charge until he came to Strabane.

A few weeks after **Mr.** Robertson's induction, the congregation took active measures in the matter of church building. At a meeting held on **October** 29th, a building **committee was appointed** consisting of Thos. **Bain, chairman ; Chas. Stewart,** John B. P. Robertson, **John Ross, Wm. Nicol, John** Rutherford, **sr., James Sanderson,** James Gray, David Brown, James L. **Robertson,** and the pastor of the church. **There is no** further record until April, 1879, when the committee met in the new church to arrange **details** regarding the pews. **In** July of the same year the sum of $2,000 was borrowed for building purposes, **and a** mortgage on the property given **as** security. **This is all** the information we get from the records of **the** time. It might be supplemented from **the** memory of those who took part in the proceedings, to the extent that **the** contract for the **stone work was** given to Mr. **Chas. Stewart, a** member of the committee, and that of the **carpenter work to** Mr. Bishop, of Jerseyville ; but for the most part, the indefiniteness and contradictory **nature** of these recollections render it inexpedient, especially **for** one who has no personal knowledge of the facts. The building itself, however, **has a** story **to tell.** The stone walls speak of the toil expended in gathering and hauling the material necessary **for** their erection, **and** there is but one opinion that this was done by the voluntary labor of the people and not included in the contract. The walls indicate also that their builders believed in a good foundation and that they dug deep in order to secure it, as the basement is more than half under ground, the entrance at the lowest corner being by a descending stairway. They also indicate that the committee did not believe in wasting money on high towers or much external ornamentation, as massiveness and solidity are the outstanding features. In shape the building is cruciform, apparently modeled after the old church with its wings attached, which would seem to suggest the strong conservative tendencies of the building committee. The size of the building (outside measurement) is 50 ft. by 81 ft. It has three entrances at the front, and in the southwest angle is the vestry which is entered from the south. The pews, circular in form, contain 400 sittings and are intersected by five aisles leading to the platform. The edifice, which is situated on the highest part of the lot, faces the east and is forty yards from the Brock Road, from which it is approached by three gates. The first opens to an avenue leading past the north side of the church to a spacious yard, surrounded on north and west by sheds and furnished with a good well and other conveniences. The second opens to a wide ascending gravel walk leading to the main entrance, which branches off on either side to the other doors. The third opens to a winding drive through the graveyard. The church was solemnly dedicated to the worship

STRABANE PRESBYTERIAN CHURCH, INTERIOR VIEW.

of God by the Rev. R. J. Laidlaw, LL. D., pastor of St. Paul's Church, Hamilton.

Mr. James Harper, sr., was ordained an elder on April 7th, 1878.

When the Hymnal of the Presbyterian Church in Canada, authorized by the General Assembly in 1881, was submitted to the congregation the same year for adoption, it was rejected by a large majority.

In the summer of 1882 there was another election of elders, which resulted in the ordination, on the 27th of October, of Messrs. David Brown, John B. P. Robertson, John Ross, Thos. McLaren, Wm. Ferrier and Alex. Nicol.

In July, 1884, the Session recorded a brief minute regarding the death of Mr. James Nicol, on June 4th, at the age of 77 years. He was a native of Aberdeenshire, Scotland, came to Canada in 1844, and three years later was ordained as one of the first elders of the church. He was a devoted and faithful member of Session. It is said of him that he was accustomed not only to observe the Sabbath with his family in the usual way by attending regularly on all the church services, but that he secured the full Sabbath day's rest for his horses as well, by giving them the Saturday afternoon's rest in lieu of the Sabbath forenoon's work in drawing the well loaded family wagon to the house of God.

In both the sessional and congregational records the designation "Nairn Church" is omitted on and after the year 1879. There is no record of the change or the cause which brought it about. The explanation given is to the effect that on account of there being a Nairn post office farther west, near Sarnia, annoyance was frequently caused by the miscarriage of letters. Also on one occasion when a minister from Toronto had been announced to lecture in Nairn Church, the audience was assembled but the lecturer failed to appear, having travelled one hundred miles farther west to a place where no one expected him. It was thought, moreover, by many, that no violence would be done to the agreement with the late Mr. Fraser, if the name "Nairn" should not be transferred to the new building, inasmuch as the old one was called by that name as long as it stood; consequently at a congregational meeting a motion was carried by which the new church was to be known in the future by the simple designation of the Strabane Presbyterian Church.

The name "Strabane" dates almost as far back as the history of the church. The early settlers at first received their mail matter at Dundas, but later on Mr. Matthew Peebles, who kept a store about half a mile south of the corner, on the Brock Road, had a post office opened there which he named after Strabane, a town in the north of Ireland, near the place of his birth. The post office was afterwards removed to a building almost opposite the church. Mr. Peebles was, for a long time one of the best known and most enterprising men in the community. Although more widely known in commercial and political life, he took considerable interest in church affairs as well.

On the 22nd of March, 1881, a special meeting of the congregation was called by the Presbytery at which Rev. Dr. Laing on behalf of the Presbytery explained that the meeting was called to ascertain the views of the congregation regarding a re-union with the congregation of Kilbride. Delegates from Kilbride also were present. After quite a number had expressed their views, some favorable and others in opposition to such an arrangement, a motion to adjourn for two weeks was carried. At the adjourned meeting the following resolution was adopted, viz.: "That while this meeting is opposed to a formal union of this congregation with that of Kilbride, yet they are willing that their minister, under the direction of Presbytery, should, during the next seven months supply the Kilbride pulpit on Sabbath afternoons and take such pastoral oversight of the congregation as the Presbytery may think fit during that time."

The annual report of 1883 shows the revenue from seat rents and plate collections to have been $755.31, collections for missions $21.

The educational facilities afforded by the Strabane public school had been suitable for the requirements of the pastor's children while young, but now the necessities of a higher education for them led Mr. Robertson to return to the vicinity of his own " alma mater " where he considered the advantages were superior to those within their reach if he were to remain here. This consideration mainly, led him to tender his resignation which was finally accepted by the Presbytery and Mr. Robertson removed to New Wilmington in the spring of 1884, where he was soon settled in another charge.

CHAPTER VI.

KILBRIDE CONGREGATION.

AT the time of Mr. McLean's removal, Kilbride was placed on the list of mission stations, and was supplied for some time by students during vacation, and occasionally during the winter months.

Rev. John Porteous of Beverley was the Moderator of Session *pro tem*. Among the students who spent a summer in Kilbride during that period were Rev. Prof. Beattie, D. D., of Columbia, S. C., and Rev. A. B. Simpson, of New York.

In 1865, Rev. James Howie was appointed as an ordained missionary for one year. The subscription list of that time shows a promise of $300 per annum for the support of ordinances.

After Mr. Howie's year had expired, the congregation took steps to extend a call, which resulted in the settlement of Mr. W. H. Simpson as pastor. The new minister was a young man, a native of Prince Edward Island, who had just graduated from Knox College. The ordination and induction took place on May 31st, 1867. Rev. David Inglis presided, and Revs. R. N. Grant and A. B. Simpson took part in the service.

The vacancy of six years proved to be a trying time to the little congregation. The members, although only forty in number, were united and hopefully looked forward to days of greater prosperity in the near future. During the following year sixteen names were added to the roll. The attitude of the Session at that time regarding church music is set forth in a resolution anent the subject, in dealing with an overture sent down by Synod for the consideration of Kirk Sessions, passed in January, 1868, viz.: " Resolved, that in view of the present state of feeling on this question, it is the opinion of this Session that the sanction by our Synod of the use of instrumental music would disturb the harmony of our church and injure the cause of Christ." Mr. Francis Small, who had been for some years past, connected with the congregation at Strabane, re-united with Kilbride, and was again inducted as a member of Session in 1869. On May 29th, 1870, W. E. Olds and Alexander Fraser were ordained to the eldership. These additions to Session were soon afterwards followed by the loss of Mr. Wilson, by death, in 1870, and the departure of Mr. Olds to the United States two years later.

On March 6th, 1873, the Session was again augmented by the addition of James Harvey and Dr. Wm. McClure. The membership at that time had increased to 71.

A glance at the business transacted by the Managers showed that in 1868 the church was

THE LATE REV. W. H. SIMPSON, D. D.

re-shingled and painted at a cost of $212. The annual report for 1871 shows that the minister was paid $516. During the same year the congregation purchased for a manse the brick cottage which had been built by Mr. McLean, and decided to advertise in *The Globe* for a precentor at $100 per annum. It will thus be observed that the prosperous times hoped for had come. The pastorate of Mr. Simpson, which seems to have been marked by harmony and progress, was suddenly terminated by his acceptance of a call to First Presbyterian Church, Madison, Indiana, on August 5th, 1873. After thirteen years of labor in the United States, his health failed and he returned to Canada, where he died in Chatham, in 1888.

Kilbride congregation, after hearing a number of probationers, extended a call to Mr. Isaac Campbell, who had just completed his studies in Knox College. Mr. Campbell was ordained and inducted on November 2nd, 1874. After a brief pastorate he accepted a call to Beverley and the charge was again declared vacant on June 11th, 1876.

Rev. E. W. Waits, of Waterdown, was appointed Moderator *pro tem*. Another season of depression was in store for this little congregation.

The mills of the Canada Powder Co., situated at Cumminsville, were closed and the plant removed to Windsor, Que. As a consequence, several families whose occupations were directly or indirectly connected with the mills, sought employment elsewhere. A number of families also withdrew from the congregation in order to unite with the church at Campbellville, where a cause had recently been established.

The few who remained held bravely together and maintained ordinances as their circumstances permitted. All proposals of union with neighboring congregations proved unsuccessful. After four years the arrangement recorded in the previous chapter was made by which Rev. Mr. Robertson of Strabane took temporary pastoral oversight and acted as Moderator of Session. An elder's certificate was forwarded to Dr. McClure who had removed from the bounds, and a minute adopted expressive of the high esteem in which he was held.

In 1883 two additional elders were elected, viz., Edward Corlett and Isaac Clugston, who were ordained on June 8th of the same year.

The Session was thus strengthened and a few were added to the membership so that the prospect began to look brighter when the removal of Rev. Mr. Robertson from Strabane again left the congregation vacant.

CHAPTER VII.

PASTORATE OF REV. J. W. CATHCART.

REV S. W. FISHER was Moderator *pro tem.* of Strabane Session during the vacancy which followed the departure of Rev. Mr. Robertson. Probationers were heard for a few months, after which Rev. Mr. Cathcart supplied the pulpit during the winter and spring.

In May the Session recorded as follows: " We hereby place on record our deep sense of appreciation of the faithful service rendered to this church by our late lamented father, Walter McFarlane, who has been a member of this Session for the past thirty-eight years, during which time he heartily identified himself with all the interests of the church, both material and spiritual. We are thankful to the Lord for sparing his servant so long to the church and for the hallowing influence of his worthy example, his earnest piety and his holy life; until, as a shock of corn fully ripe, he was gathered home on February 27th, 1885. He being dead yet speaketh."

There was a proposal to extend a call to Mr. Cathcart, but he was not eligible, not having as yet been received by the General Assembly. At the request of the people, however, the Presbytery extended his appointment with instructions that he should supply Kilbride as well.

Some of the Strabane people were disposed to propose a union with Kilbride and a meeting for the purpose was called but nothing definite accomplished. Kilbride Session appointed John Agnew to advocate union with Strabane at the coming meeting of Presbytery. Finally the Presbytery encouraging these mutual approaches, succeeded in effecting a re-union, to the evident satisfaction of all parties concerned. The united congregations then extended a call to Rev. Mr. Cathcart, which he accepted.

Mr. Cathcart was born in Waterloo County, Ont., in 1848. His parents had emigrated from Enniskillen, Ireland, the previous year and taken up land in that section, which was then a wilderness. The family belonged to the Church of England, but as the Methodists were first to carry the Gospel to the section in which they lived, they cast in their lot with that body. Mr. Cathcart grew up amid the rugged experiences of backwoods life, which has proved an excellent training to many of the most prominent professional and business men of the present time.

At the age of twenty he united with the Methodist Church and manifested such zeal in the welfare of the congregation with which he was identified that he was urged to give himself to the work of the ministry. After considerable hestation he realized that the call was from God and

REV. J. W. CATHCART.

responded "Here am I." He attended the Berlin Grammar School until he had taken a first class teacher's certificate and was received as probationer of the Methodist Church.

During the course of study prescribed for candidates for the ministry, including two sessions in college, he came in contact with the distinctive doctrines of Arminians and Calvinists, with the result that a decided preference for the Calvinistic views, as held by Presbyterians was developed in his mind. Two years later, he withdrew from the Methodist Church and was received by the Presbyterian Church in the United States, and then by that of Canada in 1885. On September 20th of the same year, he was installed as pastor of Strabane and Kilbride.

During Mr. Cathcart's pastorate the work seems to have gone forward comparatively smoothly. Special evangelistic meetings were held at Kilbride, where the attendance was much improved and the membership increased.

At Strabane the people had been devoting their energy ever since the church was built, to pay off the debt. Besides this, mainly through the personal exertion of the pastor and those who came to his assistance, the glebe was put in a much better condition and the manse was also changed both in external and internal appearance which added much to its convenience and comfort. No change in the Session at either place is recorded, with the exception of granting elders' certificates to Thomas McLaren and Alexander Nicol who removed from the bounds. There were added to the church in both places during his ministry, by profession of faith, fifty-six persons or a yearly average of fourteen.

From the latter part of Mr. Robertson's pastorate even to the present, the congregation has lost heavily by removals to Manitoba and elsewhere, so that the actual number on the roll remained about the same, notwithstanding the additions.

In the winter of 1889 Mr. Cathcart was led to tender his resignation, in order to accept a call to a church in the United States. He was released from his charge here in March of that year.

CHAPTER VIII.

PASTORATE OF REV. D. G. CAMERON.

IN November, a call was extended to the Rev. D. G. Cameron, pastor of Dungannon and Pt. Albert. The call was supported before the Presbytery of Maitland by Rev. S. Carruthers, the interim Moderator of Session, who gave reasons for the translation. The call was accepted and the present pastor was inducted at Strabane on December 24th, 1889.

Mr. Cameron was born in Osgoode, Carleton County, Ont. in 1856. His parents, who emigrated from Scotland in early life, were among the pioneers of that locality. He was brought up under the ministry of the late Rev. James Whyte, whose memory he regards with the deepest veneration. In boyhood, as the result of a fall, he passed through a severe bodily affliction, which lasted several years. During the early part of this period, he underwent a religious experience of a somewhat remarkable character. By Divine mercy, however, he emerged from this double conflict, like Jacob of old on the banks of the Jabbok.

At the age of nineteen he returned to his books and after two years in Kemptville High School, went to Montreal, where for six years he pursued the course prescribed by the Church, at McGill University and the Presbyterian College of that city, graduating from the latter institution in 1883. On the 18th of July of the same year he was licensed to preach and ordained to the work of a home missionary, in Winnipeg, by the Presbytery of Manitoba. In the autumn of 1884 he became the pastor of Erskine Church, Dungannon, where he remained until he accepted the call of Strabane and Kilbride, his present charge.

At the annual meeting in 1890 the building committee presented its final report through Mr. Jas. L. Robertson, the secretary, and after the adoption of the report, the committee was dismissed, having received the thanks of the congregation.

The report set forth that over $800 of this amount promised on subscriptions had not been paid and is therefore still due the congregation. Should this sentence be read by those to whom the statement applies, we would refer them to Deut. 23: 21, and remind them that it is not too late to make amends.

The amount received on subscription was $5547.78; from tea meetings, etc., $664.03; total, $6211.81. Expended on church building, $4979.25; repairs on manse, $282.35; sheds and stable $156.21: interest on mortgage, $794; total, $6211.81.

The Managers' account showed an expenditure of $863 for the year just closed, and that in addition

REV. D. G. CAMERON.

to the revenue, about $240 had to be borrowed to balance accounts. To this indebtedness an account of $155 was presented for board and horse hire of probationers, making at once a floating debt of about $400, which was met by special subscription.

During the summer of 1890, repairs and improvements on the interior of the Church were undertaken at a cost of over $300.

The number of communicants on the roll at the beginning of the present pastorate was 120.

The service of praise was led by a precentor and the Psalms and Paraphrases used, while at the Sunday School and evening service an organ and Gospel hymns were in use. In compliance with a request from a number of members, the Session, in 1891, submitted a ballot to the congregation in order to ascertain if they were in favor of the use of the authorized Hymnal in addition to the Psalms, and also if they were in favour of the use of an organ in the church service. The result of the vote was, for Hymnal 58, opposed 8, for Organ 48, opposed 16. The Session decided to sustain the majority of the congregation in both cases, authorize the use of the Hymnal from that date and refer the organ question to the Managers. An organ was soon purchased and a choir appointed which led the service of praise from that time.

About this time also, a change was made in the size of the Committee of Management, by which it was reduced from 20 to 6; and later the duty of taking the offering was transferred by the Session to the Managers.

A new communion set was procured, cards were substituted for the pewter tokens and a record of attendance kept.

Two deaths have occured in the Session. Mr. David Brown died on Aug. 22nd, 1894, and Mr. John Ross on Sept. 1st, 1896. They were ordained at the same time, were both about 60 years of age, intimately associated in life and not long separated by death. Regarding each, a minute was inserted in the Session record setting forth an expression of the deep sense of loss we have sustained in the removal of our departed brethren; a loss which is felt, not by the Session alone, but by the whole congregation and the community at large. Also an acknowledgment of the unflagging interest which they took in all matters pertaining to the cause of Christ, especially in connection with our own congregation, as shown in their regularity and agreeableness as well as their cheerfulness and liberality in all the services which they rendered. It was the pastor's privilege to be on the most intimate terms with these brethren in the activities of church life, and when their working days were over, to commune with them of the rest beyond; to stand on the brink as they passed over, to close their sightless eyes and commit their bodies to the earth in the sure hope of a glorious resurrection.

The vacancy caused by the death of Mr. Brown was filled by the ordination of Dr. James

McQueen, on March 3rd, 1895. Later on the congregation was asked to elect three additional elders, with the result that **Messrs** George Nicol, **Alexander** McFarlane and **Richard** Lothian were ordained on **Jan. 10th,** 1897.

The congregation during the past **seven years** has raised, on an average, for all purposes **about** $1100 a year; **of this amount an** average **of $207 a year was contributed to** missions. The communicants at present number 151.

Kilbride, during the same period, continued **to suffer losses by removals ; three families** leaving **for every one that came in,** so **that marks** of progress are scarcely to be looked **for.** An organ had been in use for several years **but not until** 1892 **was the** Hymnal introduced. **There has been no** change in the Session for 14 years. **Three years ago** the congregation improved the **appearance of** the church by **paint and** the **erection of a room at the** rear.

The union of the two congregations **twelve** years ago **has been followed by harmony and** friendship.

The Sabbath **School at Strabane dates as far** back as the **church, is comparatively well equipped,** reports 90 scholars **and over $40 in** offerings.

The Auxiliary **of the** Women's Foreign **Missionary** Society **was** organized in **1887,** and has done a good **work.**

The " White **Stone "** Mission Band **is an** enthusiastic company of youthful workers, meeting monthly to study the progress of the Church's obedience to the Saviour's command. They are not only improving their natural talents but are in possession of talent money, of which they will render an account at their annual entertainment.

The Christian Endeavor Society was organized in 1889. It has 26 active and 10 associate members, and meets weekly for prayer and Bible study. It has helped greatly in developing latent talent, and has made many improvements on church and manse which would otherwise have been left undone.

REV. JAMES BLACK.

The Rev. James Black was born in Dumfriesshire, Scotland, in 1822. He is a younger brother of the late Rev. John Black, D. D., the apostle of the Red River. His early education was received in his native land. In 1841 he came with his father's family to Bovina, State of New York. He was in 1847 enrolled as a student in Knox College. During his college course he labored for three successive summers as a student missionary in Caledonia, Allan Settlement and Oneida. On graduating, in 1853, he was ordained and inducted into the pastorate of these congregations. After laboring with fidelity and success in this charge for upwards of thirty-six years, he resigned and came to live in Hamilton. Having given temporary supply for a few years to various congregations, he retired from the active work of the ministry by permission of the General Assembly. Mr. Black occupies a high place in the love and esteem of his brethren in the ministry, whose fond hope is that the "Venerable Father of the Presbytery" may be continued with them for many years.

CHAPTER IX.

THE JUBILEE.

AT a meeting of Session held in January last, attention was drawn to the fact that the 19th of March would be the fiftieth anniversary of the organization of the congregation. The Session concluded that some action should be taken to observe the event in a becoming manner. At a subsequent meeting it was decided that on account of the usual bad state of the roads at that season, it would be better to have the celebration on the 12th of May, on which date, fifty years ago, the Presbytery of Hamilton ratified the action of those who were appointed to effect the organization. A programme of the services was prepared and circulated, the carrying out of which affords material for this chapter.

Service preparatory to the Communion was conducted on May 7th, by Rev. W Robertson of Morriston, who preached an excellent sermon from Heb. 13 : 8, "Jesus Christ the same yesterday, to-day and forever." Although not specially arranged, this service, at which six members were received, was a fitting commencement to the series of meetings which followed.

Sabbath morning, May 9th, was fair, and a large congregation assembled to worship the God of their fathers. The Venerable Dr. Wardrope conducted the service. After prayer, the pastor announced the 35th Paraphrase and requested that it should be sung without the use of the organ, and that the congregation should remain seated as in bygone days. Dr. Wardrope addressed the communicants and dispensed the bread, and the pastor dispensed the wine and conducted the closing exercises. The six elders of Strabane officiated, and the elders from Kilbride sat with them on the platform. A season of blessed communion was enjoyed by those who were present.

In the afternoon a service of praise and thanksgiving was conducted by the pastor, at which Dr. Wardrope again delivered an earnest and touching address on "Consecration."

In the evening the Rev. John Young, M. A., pastor of St. John's Church, Hamilton, conducted the service.

On Wednesday afternoon, May 12th, the audience was not so large as expected, partly, no doubt, on account of the busy season. The pastor presided, and with him on the lower platform were the two representatives from the Presbytery and Dr. Wardrope. On the upper platform were five of the neighboring ministers, Mr. Flatt, M. P. P., of Hamilton, and Dr. McQueen, of Freelton. After devotional exercises and a few introductory remarks, the chairman read a letter from Mr.

Thomas Bain, M. P., in which he expressed regret that an urgent business engagement detained him in Ottawa; otherwise he would have been with his friends in Strabane, where he had spent the best part of his life. Letters of congratulation were received from Revs. J. L. Robertson and J. W. Cathcart, former pastors, Revs. D. Wardrope, D. W. Fisher, H. N. Hall, A. Stewart and J. Mahaffy, and Messrs. E. S. Bronson, J. R. Robertson, W. M. Robertson, A. Andrew, and Drs. Addison and Shanks. From notes of the addresses taken by Mr. Corrigal, Principal of our school, we are able to give a brief epitome.

Dr. McQueen read the first two chapters of the historical sketch, after which the chairman called upon Rev. James Black, the *father* of the Presbytery of Hamilton, who said it afforded him great pleasure to convey to the congregation the greetings of the Presbytery on this very interesting occasion. Of the ministers belonging to the Presbytery which organized this congregation fifty years ago, not one remained. The bounds of the Presbytery at that time were much larger than now, extending from Lake Erie to the Georgian Bay. His connection with the Presbytery dated almost as far back as the event they were commemorating. His knowledge of Strabane was not of recent date, for through two of his fellow students, George and David Wardrope, he knew of their father's home and work in this locality. He had been well acquainted with Mr. McLean and also with Messrs. Robertson and Cathcart and wished to express his high regard for the present devoted pastor. He closed with an appeal to the present members to follow in the footsteps of their fathers, as far as these were in the right direction, to keep up the missionary spirit, to preserve peace and union, and to support the efforts of their pastor.

Rev. Dr. Wardrope, the *father* of the Presbytery of Guelph, made a few friendly remarks and stated that as he had addressed the congregation twice already, he would make way for the other brethren.

Rev. Dr. Fletcher, of Hamilton, who was associated with Mr. Black in conveying the greetings of the Presbytery, was the next speaker. He said he had listened with great interest to the paper read by Dr. McQueen, and that they were doing well to preserve and honor the memory of their fathers who had been the pioneers of this new country. He spoke of the struggles and privations of the early settlers and recalled some of his own experiences as a missionary. He had stayed over night with a settler and his family in a shanty that contained only one room. While in bed a heavy rainstorm came on and he had to make use of his umbrella in order to keep himself dry. He had been for twenty-five years a member of the Presbytery and had no sympathy with the modern idea that a minister passes the "dead line" at fifty. After paying a tribute to the godly life

REV. D H. FLETCHER, D. D.

Rev. Dr. Fletcher is a native of Scotland, where his early academical studies were commenced, and which were subsequently prosecuted at Toronto University and Knox College. Graduating in 1860, he was settled the same year at Scarboro. There he continued to labor with marked success till called, in 1872, to his present charge in Hamilton. His congregation recently celebrating the semi-jubilee of his induction into the McNab Street Church, expressed in a most cordial and tangible form their appreciation of his worth and services. His Alma Mater, in recognition of his attainments and services, conferred on him the degree of D. D. Dr. Fletcher has been Moderator of the Synod of Hamilton and London, and has rendered good service to the Church as an examiner in Knox College and a member of its Board of Management.

and character of the late Mr. McLean and kindly reference to his successors, he closed by giving some good advice to the congregation.

Mr. Flatt in his address said that most of the names recalled were familiar to him, as he had bought the timber on nearly all the farms in this part of the country. After describing the condition of the country in those days and the hardships of the early settlers, he addressed the young people present and urged upon them more perseverence. They knew nothing of hard times. If they made half the effort their fathers had made they would succeed. He spoke of walking to Dundas, from Millgrove, and carrying fifty pounds of flour home on his back. Dr. Wardrope who was just leaving, supplemented Mr. Flatt's experience by stating that when he was a boy he walked from Puslinch to Dundas and back in a day, nearly forty miles in all, and carried a cross-cut-saw seven feet long.

Revs. W. Robertson, F. Ballantyne, P. M. McEachern, H. E. Hill and W. Spencer, the pastor's nearest ministerial neighbors, all made brief and pointed speeches expressive of good feeling and brotherly kindness.

In the audience a few survivors of the early days were noticed, viz., James Sanderson, who helped to build the first church, Mrs. Reid, who was a member at the time of organization, and Mr. McBeth, of Puslinch, who travelled the Brock Road in 1830.

At the close of the meeting a photograph was taken of the church and a goodly number of those present formed a group at the north-east angle. A reproduction of the picture is here given as well as interior view looking in the same direction.

On the same evening at 8 o'clock a concert was held at which there was a good attendance. Mrs. McArthur of Hamilton was the singer, and Mr. J. W. Bengough of Toronto, the speaker.

The morning and evening services on Sabbath, May 16th, were conducted by Rev. Dr. McKay of Woodstock. At the conclusion of the morning service, three children were baptized, viz.: George Edward Rutherford, William Stanley Rodgers and Edith Galloway.

On the following Sabbath morning the pastor preached from Phil. 3 : 13-14, " Forgetting those things which are behind and reaching forth unto those things which are before, etc." He reviewed the events of the past two weeks, spoke of the eternity of memory, pointed out that while God's goodness should always be remembered, there were many things which should, if possible, be forgotten, and that the text indicated that the best way to unburden the memory of the worthless and injurious recollections of the past, was to keep the present fully occupied in the performance of those duties and the practice of those virtues which ensure not only pleasant memories for others but a blessed realization of Divine favor to ourselves.

STRABANE PRESBYTERIAN CHURCH, EXTERIOR VIEW.

Remembrance of God's Benefits.

Sermon preached by Rev. Thomas Wardrope, D. D., on Sabbath morning, May 9th, 1897.

PSALM 116 : 12-14—"What shall I render unto the Lord for all His benefits toward me? I will take the cup of salvation, and call upon the name of the Lord. I will pay my vows unto the Lord now in the presence of all His people."

IT is not well with our souls when we fail to recognize the hand of the Lord in His dealings with us. It is not well with us, when we can survey the works of His hands, when we can partake of the bounties of His providence, when we can retire to rest at night and awake with new strength in the morning, without any feeling of love or gratitude to Him who "opens His hand and satisfies the desire of every living thing." It was not so with the Psalmist. He recalled God's mercies to his recollection with gratitude and joy: "Bless the Lord, O my soul, and all that is within me, bless His holy name." With wonder, too, he thought of them, and with the conviction that blessings so varied and so innumerable should be acknowledged by some becoming return in the way of loving devotion. "What shall I render unto the Lord for all His benefits toward me?"

This utterance of the Psalmist was indited by the Holy Spirit, who works in the hearts of God's people, producing in them right emotions, awakening in them right desires, and prompting them to seek communion with God, in meditation alike upon the works of His hands and upon the revelation of His holy will. This being so, the language of this psalm becomes ours, when we appropriate it, as really as it was that of the Psalmist. And we have a right to appropriate it. The word of God is given to us, with all its gracious invitations and all its precious promises—given to us, that we may make it our own; and the more we express our petitions and our thanksgivings in the very words which it contains, so much the more do we fall in with the gracious design of Him who has given it to us. The circumstances in which we are met to-day concur with our text in teaching us to reflect, in the first place, upon the blessings which God bestows; and in the second place, upon the inquiry which the remembrance of these blessings suggests.

I. The blessings which God bestows: "All His benefits." Many of these blessings are referred to in the Psalms, and more are suggested by their inspired words: "O, how great is Thy goodness which Thou hast laid up in store for them that fear Thee; which Thou hast wrought for them that trust in Thee before the sons of men!" On the pages of revelation we see some enumeration of them; but, if our eyes are open, we can see them recorded too on the pages of our own memory and experience. In what we have ourselves seen and known and experienced of the goodness of the Lord, we find abundant cause for the ascription of praise: "How precious are Thy thoughts unto me, O God! how great is the sum of them! If I should count them, they are more in number than the sand: when I awake I am still with Thee."

We cannot reckon them up. God's people, as has been well said, "should do with their mercies as botanists do with their flowers—classify them; or as astronomers do with the stars—group them in constellations. Take a retrospect of mercies temporal and spiritual, mercies public and private, mercies personal and relative. Think of continued mercies, of restored mercies, of preventing and delivering mercies. Fix your minds on particular instances; for instances affect much more powerfully than things in a mass. Do not overlook the circumstances which enhance the benefits you have received: give due place to thoughts suggested by their seasonableness, their utility, their preciousness."

God has been blessing you, my friends, all your lives long; and that, in a very real sense, whether you have valued His guidance and protection or not. What innumerable blessings has God bestowed upon you, altogether irrespective of the "spiritual blessings in heavenly places" with which He blesses His own people in Christ Jesus! How has He blessed you in His providence! Health and strength, food and raiment, home and friends—all that you enjoy, you owe to Him.

For the land you live in, you may well give thanks to God. Could you be transplanted, even for a week, to a heathen country, without the knowledge of God, without the Gospel of Christ, without the ordinances of worship, without the benefits of a Christian civilization, you might be more ready to say, with reference to your own land, "The lines are fallen unto me in pleasant places; yea, I have a goodly heritage." For the healthfulness of your climate, for the fertility of your fields, for the benefits of constitutional government, for the efficiency of your municipal institutions, for the excellence of your educational system, for all the privileges of a free country, you are indebted to Him, the Giver of all good.

But it is almost impossible to speak of the temporal mercies bestowed upon you, and to dissociate from them the mention of the spiritual privileges with which God has favoured you. Those of you who have fallen in with God's offers of mercy, and tasted of the riches of His grace, I may well call upon you to reflect, with adoring wonder, on the provision that God has made for the wants of your souls. "All His benefits!" How much else He has given us you have been reminded; but besides all, and above all, He has given His "unspeakable gift"—that, without which all else would have been comparatively valueless—"His only begotten Son, that whosoever believeth in Him should not perish, but have everlasting life."

The beloved disciple, taught of God, knew, as few men know, how to estimate every gift of His love. In the miracle at Cana of Galilee, in the healing of the sick, in the cleansing of the lepers, in the feeding of the five thousand, in the miraculous draught of fishes, in the kind, but so familiar question, "Children, have ye any meat?" and in all else like this that he saw and heard, he had seen wonderful proofs of the Divine love. But when he comes to the great and unspeakable gift, all else becomes as nothing in comparison with this. "Herein is love," he says, as if comparatively no love had been manifested in any other of the works and ways of God: "Herein is love, not that we loved God, but that He loved us, and sent His Son to be the propitiation for our sins." For this the apostle of the Gentiles offers the wonderful prayer: Even for this, "That Christ may dwell in your hearts by faith; that ye, being rooted and grounded in love, may be able to comprehend with all saints, what is the breadth, and length, and depth, and height; and to know the love of Christ, which passeth knowledge, that ye might be filled with all the fulness of God." Let us seek then to-day, gathered as we are for this service of commemoration and thanksgiving, that our hearts may be lifted up in adoration and praise, as we hear the word that comes to us, through inspiration of the Holy Ghost, " Behold, what manner of love the Father hath bestowed on us, that we should be called the sons of God . . . Beloved, now are we the sons of God ; and it doth not yet appear what we shall be : but we know that, when He shall appear, we shall be like Him ; for we shall see Him as He is. And every man that hath this hope in Him purifieth himself, even as He is pure."

But I must now refer more particularly to the scenes witnessed in by-gone days, and the vicissitudes experienced, by you to whom I speak this morning, and by those who went before you. With few, if any, exceptions, the pioneers of this settlement have passed away from this earthly scene ; but many of you can well remember fathers and mothers who, in their prime, left the old land, the cherished home of their childhood and youth, to seek a dwelling-place in the then comparatively unknown colony of Canada. And all of you know, if not from memory, at any rate from family tradition, the privations that they had to endure, the toil with which they wrought, the difficulties with which they had to contend, as they hewed out in the forest homes for themselves and for their children. God has so blessed the labor of their hands, that now, on every side, there are comfortable houses where the original "shanties" stood; there are well-tilled farms where, within the memory of some of you, trees of gigantic growth reared their towering summits

REV. THOMAS WARDROPE, D. D.

Rev. Dr. Wardrope was born at Ladykirk, Scotland, May 16th, 1819, was educated in Ladykirk Parish School, at Edinburgh University and Queen's College, Kingston. He was pastor of Knox Church, Ottawa, 1845-1869, and of Chalmers Church, Guelph, 1869-1892, when he retired from the pastorate. In 1878 Queen's University conferred on him the degree of D. D. He was Convener of the Assembly's Foreign Mission Committee from 1884 to 1891. The highest honor in the gift of the Church was bestowed on him in 1891 when he was elected as Moderator of the General Assembly. Being free from the responsibility of a pastor and in the enjoyment of excellent health, he is enabled to respond to many invitations, where his services are always appreciated, and at the manses of his younger brethren a visit from him is regarded as a benediction.

toward the clouds; and there are well made roads where the early settlers found their way by following a "blaze" through the bush. Those who can remember what the Brock Road was fifty years ago, the rude huts in which the first in-comers lived when they were laboriously making their little clearings, and the crops growing among stumps or among "girdled" trees, will understand how truly we may say, "The wilderness and the solitary place has been made glad, and the desert has been made to rejoice and blossom as the rose."

Some of you can remember, too, the first efforts made to gather a little company for worship, near the very spot on which this building stands. There were a few who cherished hallowed memories of Sabbaths and Sabbath services in the old homes beyond the sea, and wondered if they should ever again be made glad by its being said to them, "Let us go into the house of the Lord." They gathered together sometimes for a Sabbath School, sometimes for a prayer meeting, sometimes to hear the word from a missionary or an evangelist turning in to abide with them for the night, or over the Sabbath day. And they gladly welcomed men of various denominations, and with different ways of presenting the truth, but all taught by the one Spirit, and constrained by the love of the same Saviour—they gladly welcomed them and eagerly listened to them as they preached the Gospel of the grace of God. Then gradually organization became more complete, and the first building for the use of the Presbyterian Church was erected. The services held in it many of you will remember, and look back upon with gratitude and joy. And now, to this house, more commodious, and more in keeping with your surroundings, you repair from Sabbath to Sabbath, with this purpose in your hearts, "We will go into His tabernacles, we will worship at His footstool;" and with this conviction, based upon God's word, and confirmed by your own experience, "A day in Thy courts is better than a thousand; I had rather be a doorkeeper in the house of my God, than to dwell in the tents of wickedness." "Blessed is the man whom Thou choosest, and causest to approach unto Thee, that he may dwell in Thy courts; we shall be satisfied with the goodness of Thy house, even of Thy holy temple."

Now look back on the way by which the Lord your God has led you. Consider how He has blessed your congregation from the day of its small beginnings until now. Remember his gracious dealings with you as individuals, as families, as a congregation. It is well to review the past. There are milestones, as we may call them, along the path which has been trodden by every child of God—Bethels, Peniels, Ebenezers, where God has been called upon in faith, and found to be a very present help in trouble. Are there not pillars set up here and there, along the pathway of your lives, marking out places and times which you can never forget, known in many cases only to your own hearts and to God? If you have been careful to set up such pillars, you will understand much of the faithfulness, and wisdom, and love, which have marked God's dealings with you. And if there are no such stones of memorial set up along the way by which you have journeyed, O what utter blanks—what deserts—spiritually, your lives must have been! If there are no such stones of memorial, it is not because you have had no reason for the erection of them, but because you have not been wise, nor observed these things, not understood the loving-kindness of the Lord. You have lived as destitute of the knowledge of God, as if the heavens had ceased to declare His glory, and the firmament to show His handiwork. You have lived just as if there were no Saviour, and no need of a Saviour—as if God had never sent His Son that, in Him you might "have redemption through His blood, the forgiveness of sins according to the riches of His grace."

II. The inquiry which the remembrance of God's benefits suggests, "What shall I render unto the Lord for all his benefits toward me?" What a profoundly suggestive word is this, in which we find the Psalmist saying, "O my soul, forget not all His benefits!" If he, the man according to God's own heart, so specially taught by the Holy Spirit, thus deeply felt the necessity of admonishing, of stirring up, his own soul, may not we, every one of us, when reflecting upon God's benefits, well say,

"O my soul, forget them not?" May we not well hear the word as addressed to us, "Now therefore stand still, that I may reason with you before the Lord of all the righteous acts of the Lord, which He did to you and to your fathers." Let us summon ourselves into God's presence. Let us attend to the inspired writer, as he reasons with us " before the Lord." Let us remember how the Lord, by the dispensations of His providence, b, the instructions of His word, by the admonitions of our own consciences, by the promptings and strivings of His Holy Spirit, has sought to bring us into blessed communion with himself. So much has He done, with this gracious end in view, that I cannot answer, and you cannot answer, when He appeals to us, and says, "What more could have been done?"

Look back, my dear friends, I say again. Retrace in thought the way by which you have been led. Remember how God made that crooked path straight; how He made that rough way smooth. Remember how, in perplexity, He gave you counsel, how in affliction he gave you comfort. Remember how, when calamities threatened, the time which you had most dreaded passed by, and yet the calamities did not overwhelm you. What cause have you to say, "He hath delivered my soul from death, mine eyes from tears, and my feet from falling."

And now observe how closely connected with his inquiry what he should render to the Lord for all His benefits was the Psalmist's resolution to render some return. A return, in the way of recompense, he knew he could never render. He never thought of any such thing. No such thing does God expect or require from any of us. What He gives, He gives freely, "without money and without price." But the Psalmist knew that he could render, and that God expected—and, best of all, that God would value—some return in the way of grateful and loving devotion. What then shall we render? This question arises spontaneously in our minds, and full of a peculiar significance, at the communion table.

This, the ordinance of the Lord's Supper, is one of commemoration. And on this day, of so many hallowed memories, we specially remember, and in His own appointed way commemorate, the finished work of our Lord and Saviour Jesus Christ. The atoning sacrifice of Christ is ever to be commemorated by the ordinance which we observe to-day. In all ages and in all lands this feast is to be celebrated till our Lord shall come. This has superseded the ordinance of the Passover: "Christ our Passover is sacrificed for us." That prefigured the redemption of His people by the shedding of blood—this turns our thoughts towards the redemption now accomplished.

This ordinance is one of instruction. It turns our attention to the fact of Christ's death, to the manner of His death, to the cause of His death, and to the certainty of His coming again. "Ye do show the Lord's death till He come." We, seated at this table, commemorating His dying love, doing this in remembrance of Him, hear His word: "I will come again, and receive ye unto myself." Here we wait, "looking for that blessed hope, and the glorious appearing of the great God, even our Saviour, Jesus Christ"—the hour when "The Lord Himself shall descend from heaven with a shout, with the voice of the archangel and the trump of God, and the dead in Christ shall rise first. Then we that are alive and remain shall be caught up together with them in the clouds to meet the Lord in the air, and so shall we ever be with the Lord. Wherefore comfort one another with these words."

This ordinance is one of communion. It not only commemorates what Christ has done, and instructs us as to the relation which Christ sustains to His people, but is a channel of communication whereby in many instances are conveyed to Christ's people the richest blessings of His grace. Hence it is called, by way of eminence, "the communion"; and returning sacramental occasions are called "communion seasons." The cup of blessing, which we bless, is it not the communion of the blood of Christ? The bread which we break, is it not the communion of the body of Christ? It is so in reality with Christ's people. Others come and receive nothing, because they ask nothing, desire nothing, expect nothing; but those who come, hungering and thirsting after the blessings therein set forth, are "by faith made partakers of His body and blood, with all His benefits, to their spiritual nourishment and growth in grace."

This ordinance is one of consolation. The disciples were in great sorrow when it was instituted; and the Lord graciously remembered and recognized their need of consolation. " Let not your heart be troubled." At many times and in many ways of which we cannot now speak, Christ comforts His people. With peculiarly rich consolation does He bless them, many a time, at the table of communion. "I go to my Father," He says. "In my Father's house are many mansions. I go to prepare a place for you. I will see you again and your hearts shall rejoice; and your joy no man taketh from you. Peace I leave with you, my peace I give unto you. These things have I spoken unto you, that my joy might remain in you, and that your joy might be full."

This ordinance is one of consecration, renewed consecration of ourselves to God. It is all important that, resting on the atonement and intercession of Christ, and in humble dependence on the grace of the Holy Spirit, we should willingly and deliberately yield ourselves to God. You and I may remember a day, an hour (whether at the first coming to Christ or not), when we did most specially say to our Lord, in a way never to be forgotten, "I give myself to thee." And this may well be repeated, this consecration of ourselves may well be renewed, at the Lord's table, although certainly to the Lord's table it should not be confined. I give myself to Thee, whose I am, in this hour, to be taught, to be upheld, to be employed, to be led in the way everlasting.

> "'Tis done, the great transaction's done,
> I am my Lord's, and He is mine:
> He drew me and I followed on,
> Charmed to confess the voice Divine."

This brings us again to the question of our text, "What shall I render to the Lord for all His benefits?" I ask you to remember this—that the purposes which you form in reference to a diligent and loving observance of God's ordinances, and a cheerful obedience to His will—the purposes that you form, in full view and under a deep sense of what He has done for you—are the right purposes. These are the purposes that you should prayerfully seek to carry out, even when the impressions produced upon your minds may in some measure have faded away. In your daily life, when weary with work, when harassed with care, when assailed by temptation, when mourning under bereavement, look to the Lord as your rest, your comfort, your portion forever. Hear the word as spoken to you: "Be ye steadfast, unmoveable, always abounding in the work of the Lord, forasmuch as ye know that your labor is not in vain in the Lord." Amen.

JAMES SANDERSON.

DR. McQUEEN.   WILLIAM FERRIER.

Present Elders of Strabane.

GEORGE NICOL.

ALEXANDER McFARLANE. RICHARD LOTHIAN.

Present Elders of Strabane.

Reverence my Sanctuary.

Sermon preached by Rev John Young, M. A., of St. John Church, Hamilton, on Sabbath evening, May 9th, 1897.

LEVITICUS 26 : 2.

ON one occasion Bacon made the following statement: "I have no difficulty in satisfying my mind as to one Creator. The beautiful harmony in nature bespeaks but one great Designer and Creator. The will of that Creator I find expressed in the Bible. The same mind is expressed in the Bible as is expressed in nature." Further, Bacon said: "I met that Creator in His own house. Reverently I entered God's house, and there I met Him as He has promised to meet all devout worshippers."

To-day we shall consider what is meant by reverencing God's house. Much depends upon reverence. Whether our worship will prove helpful or not, depends largely upon our frame of mind while in the sanctuary. The reverent worshipper is sure to meet God. The irreverent worshipper is denied that great delight.

But what does reverence mean? We turn to the word of God and there we learn. In reverence we find a threefold idea: First we have the element of fear, and yet we must be careful to discriminate, for there are different kinds of fear. In Proverbs 29:25, we read that "The fear of man bringeth a snare." Here we have reference to that fear which a slave might entertain of his master. He feels that he is under his master, and that his master may abuse or illtreat him. Such a fear is crushing and depressing. Again, in II. Chronicles 14:14, we have reference to fear awakened by another motive. Here we read that Asa, King of Israel, destroyed "all the cities round about Gerar; for the fear of the Lord came upon them." These inhabitants felt that they were in opposition to Israel's God. They did not wish to comply with God's way. Their own way they preferred, and desired to overthrow the people of Jehovah. Now that they are defeated, they feared God. They felt that they had done wrong, and that they were deserving of punishment. A similar fear was entertained by the Israelites themselves when the book of Deuteronomy was read in the days of Josiah's reign. This book denounced the sins of the people, and predicted the terrible judgments which were to be meted out to the guilty. When the people learned of the blessings that were attached to obedience, and the punishments that were attached to disobedience, they feared. They felt guilty, and knew that Jehovah was able to visit them with His terrible curses. Now this is not the fear suggested by the word reverence. Nor is it the fear suggested by the authority and abuse of a slave master. Both of those kinds of fear point downward. They are of the flesh fleshy.

The fear suggested by the term reverence is that referred to in the 19th psalm and 9th verse "The fear of the Lord is clean." It is a fear that exalts, helps. The worshipper knows God to be pure and holy. Sin He abhors. The worshipper realizes that he himself is prone to evil. Coming in to the house of God he is afraid that he may take in something that will provoke God's displeasure. He is anxious to meet Jehovah. He desires to be pure and chaste, so that his meeting will be a delight and a help. Love brings him into the house of prayer. A knowledge of God's nature awakens a dread lest he may soil or defile the sacredness of the sanctuary. The same fear was entertained by a Scotchman who visited Niagara Falls some time ago. After being lowered to the gorge below, he removed his hat. "Why do you uncover your head?" asked the guide. "I feel," replied the old man, "that I am in the presence of Jehovah, for never before did I witness such a display of His majesty." He feared God, and the place where God appeared to him, he reverenced.

In this attitude we should approach God's house. Everything that might soil or taint, we should leave behind. Malice should be kept out; jealousy, illwill, pride and the like are offensive to God, and will soil the sanctuary. He who reverences God's house will not bring anything objectionable into its sacred precincts. He will fear God and will enter His house with that fear which elevates and quickens and fits for associating with the King of Kings.

The second element we notice in reverence is the element of "bowing down." Careful investigation will reveal to us that the bowing is suggested by different motives. Illustrations will reveal more clearly what is meant. When Abraham was bereaved of Sarah, he sought a burial place. Having no ground which he could call his own, he made a request of the sons of Heth, saying, "I am a stranger and a sojourner with you; give me a possession of a burying place with you, that I may bury my dead out of my sight." The children of Heth answered Abraham: "Hear us, my Lord, thou art a mighty prince among us, in the choice of our sepulchre bury thy dead. "And Abraham stood up and bowed himself to the people of the land." He felt indebted to the sons of Heth. They could have denied him his request They were under no obligations to him. Abraham appreciated the favor, and hence bowed out of gratitude. So, too, will the reverend worshipper bow in the house of God. He will realize his indebtedness to Jehovah. Not one favor, but many favors received from the Lord will rise before his mind. Those favors he cannot repay, although they were so much needed. They were beyond the giving of man, and culminated

REV. JOHN YOUNG, M. A,

Rev. John Young, M. A., is a son of Mr. Alex Young, one of the surviving pioneers of Colborne Township, Huron County, Ont., who settled there in 1833, and who has been for more than half a century a worthy elder of the Presbyterian Church. Rev. Mr. Young is a graduate in the arts, and in theology, of Queen's College, Kingston. After a post-graduate course of two years in Edinburgh, he returned to Canada and was ordained as pastor of Niagara Falls South. After a successful pastorate of five years, he was called to St. Enoch's Church, Toronto, where he remained three years, until called to St. John Church, Hamilton, his present charge, in 1895. Besides ministering to an important city congregation, Mr. Young is rendering valuable service in Christian work of a more general character.

in Christ, a Saviour of man. The true worshipper enters God's house with a deep sense of indebtedness, and feeling his own poverty, bows out of sincere gratitude, and by his very act says, "I thank Thee, oh God, for Thy many favors."

Nor is this idea exhausted when we speak of this bowing from gratitude. Another element suggests a humble attitude in God's house.

When David came to the throne, he sought out the relatives of Saul, his predecessor, that he might do them honor. Mephibosheth, Jonathan's son, was brought into his presence. His being brought to the king's palace aroused suspicions in the mind of the poor cripple. He knew that Saul had ill-treated David, and now he feared that David might take vengeance upon Saul's relatives. Although unwilling to appear at the palace, he is obliged to obey the king's mandate. When he met the king, kindness and friendship were experienced, instead of punishment and injury, and on ascertaining that the new king meant good to all the relatives of Saul, Mephibosheth surrendered himself completely to David, and bowing in his presence, he offered no resistance whatsoever. He bowed, being desirous to yield himself completely to the king.

The true worshipper will be pleased to recognize the authority of the King of kings. He will humbly bow at His footstool, feeling that former disobedience should merit punishment and banishment. Glad of the opportunity, however, he surrenders unconditionally, and promises loyalty and devotion.

He who reverences the house of God will not only bow out of gratitude and out of a desire to surrender completely to Jehovah, but will bow from another motive, such a motive as prompted Judah to bow in the presence of Joseph. When the messenger from Joseph overtook Judah and his brethren, he charged them with theft. The silver cup belonging to the king was missing, and some one in Judah's party had the cup. Judah denied the charge and became very indignant. A search was made, and the missing cup was found in Benjamin's bag, to the great humiliation of the eldest brother. Greatly mortified, they all returned to the Egyptian court. On meeting Joseph, who was yet unknown to him, Judah made a clean breast of the whole charge. "The cup was found in Benjamin's sack. We acknowledge the whole affair. We keep nothing back. We are guilty," and he bowed himself to the ground. Out of confession he bowed, because he realized the wrong.

He who reverences the sanctuary of Jehovah will see his own sins. The guilt of his iniquities and transgressions will rise before him in a most serious form, and like Judah, he will willingly confess them all. His prayer will be: "Pardon mine iniquities, O Lord, for they are very great." I am guilty, very guilty, but I make a full confession. I hide nothing from Thee. All my sins, my iniquities, my transgressions, I confess. **Lord receive and forgive.**

The **third** element we notice in reverence is that of *entering in*. Not long ago we visited a town in Ontario. A new High school had been erected a short time before. On going over to visit the school, a **student of the school drew near.** From him we learned considerable **about the institution**. We stood without and admired the building. From the reputation of the teachers we were justified in commending the **school. The** building, **the** teachers, **the order, indeed** everything about the institution **was** satisfactory. The student went in and **took part in the** studies. He imbibed the spirit **of the institution.** The truth taught became his. **His whole life** was changed by his association **with that school.** His **attitude was** very different **from that** of the visitors.

He who stands without and admires the **church building, speaks well** of pastor and people, **believes the truth is taught in that church** building, **may not reverence the house of God. He requires** to **go in, to receive the truth taught, imbibe** the **spirit of the church, put on the character of the Great Head of the** church and **grow unto His** blessed image. **He must** become identified therewith **and appropriate the** truth expounded from time to **time. In this way he sees** Jehovah, **associates** with Him, **and receives at His** hand **that** which will enlighten **and subdue.**

He who reverences God's house will *fear* the

house, will *bow down* in the house, and will *enter in* to the house. Not that there is anything sacred in the mere building. Bricks and mortar and timber are not holy things. Only intelligent beings are sacred Only persons who have "put on Christ" are sacred. The building is to be reverenced only because of the presence of Jehovah. He is holy, and it is because He has promised to be present, is the house to be characterized by reverence. All who thus reverence the sanctuary shall not be disappointed in coming to the house of God. The sermon may not be an able production, the music may be poor, the prayers offered may be faulty, but he who really reverences the sanctuary shall not come in vain.

JOHN AGNEW.

ALEXANDER FRASER.

EDWARD CORLETT.

ISAAC CLUGSTON.

Present Elders of Kilbride.

The Worship of God in our Families.

The Sermon preached in the Church, Strabane, on Sabbath morning, May 16th, 1897, by Rev. W. A. Mackay, B. A., D. D., Woodstock, Ont.

TEXT.—Joshua 24 : 15.
"As for me and my house we will serve the Lord."

FROM this text I wish to speak to you on the duty of worshipping God in our homes, a very important practical duty, and one which I trust will be in accord with the solemn services in which you have already been engaged on this happy occasion. You have been celebrating your jubilee. And it must have been very pleasant to recount the goodness of the Lord to you, these fifty years. You have had your trials, but you have also had your triumphs; and looking at your trials in the light of to-day, I trust you will find they were only blessings in disguise. Hitherto hath the Lord helped you.

But we cannot live on memories. The bread we ate last year will not do us to-day. The sunshine of last summer will not paint the flowers of this summer. The study of the past is profitable only when it leads to greater earnestness in improving the living present. May God help me to speak, and you to hear, so that the resolution of our text will be the determination of our hearts on entering another important epoch of your history as a congregation.

Home! Who can estimate its influence for weal or for woe through time and eternity! There the first and strongest impressions are made, and an education insensibly gained which schools can never supply, nor after-influences ever efface. The family is God's institution; and for more than two thousand five hundred years after the fall, the knowledge of the true God was preserved among men chiefly by heads of families. And still the family is the unit of society. "Out of families nations are spun," says Luther, the great reformer. The character of the Church, as well as of the nation, is determined in the family. In the long and absolute dependence of children upon their parents for the supply of nearly every want, God surely teaches us how sacred is the trust that lies in the mother's gentle arms, and claims the father's tenderest care. The young lamb and the little nestling, with the whole animal creation, soon learn to take care of themselves; but the immortal child is first an helpless babe, and long an infant in body and mind, thrown upon the warm bosom of maternal love, a delicate, sensitive, precious being, the charm of the household—the gift of a beneficent God, to be nourished and brought up in His fear and for His glory.

Would we, then, efficiently carry out the Divine purposes, we must put ourselves in harmony with the Divine plan. We must begin our work where

God begins it, not in the world, nor in the Sabbath school, nor even in the church, but in the home; praying that God would, in His mercy, "turn the hearts of the fathers to the children, and the hearts of the children to their fathers."

In the prevailing lack of family religion throughout our land, we find a sufficient though a sad explanation of the youthful indifference and irreligion which we deplore. Young persons come to the church, the Sunday school, or the Bible class, and they are taught the supreme claims of religion, and the duty and privilege of professing faith in Christ. But they go home and see their parents who, perhaps, are members of the church, as selfish and worldly, as proud and peevish and violent in their temper, as those who make no profession of religion. If the form of family worship is kept up it is gone through in a cold, heartless way that produces disgust in the minds of the young. The public ordinances of religion, such as the mid-week prayer meeting, the Sabbath assembly, or even the observance of the Lord's supper, are for the most trivial excuses neglected. The testimony of the home, in not a few cases, virtually give the lie to the teaching of the church. Is it surprising that under such home influences so many young persons soon come to regard religion with indifference, and all public profession of it with positive aversion; not a few living as if God were a myth, heaven a dream, the atonement a cheat, and eternity nothing?

Looking at the duty of family worship more in detail, let us observe

I. Its obligations.

II. Its benefits.

III. The difficulties frequently urged for the non-observance of it.

I. The obligation of family worship may be clearly inferred from the example of holy men in every age of the Church. Look at Abraham, the father of the faithful and the friend of God. His family religion is that for which he is specially blessed by God. In Genesis 18: 19, the Lord says, "I know Abraham that he will command his children and his household after him; and they shall keep the way of the Lord, to do justice and judgment, that the Lord may bring upon Abraham that which He hath spoken of him." Abraham is here commended for instructing his children and his household (1) "in the way of the Lord," that is the great doctrines of religion; and (2) in "doing justice and judgment," that is, in the great duties of religion. And observe, "he will command" them; that is, he will, in a proper way, use his authority as the head of a family in the religious instruction of his children. Abraham also prayed with his family. Wherever he fixed his tent, there he built an altar to the Lord and called upon the name of the Lord. Now all true believers are the children of Abraham, and if so they will do the works of Abraham. The neglect of family worship, therefore, indicates that those neglecting it do not belong to Christ.

The altar which Isaac erected at Beersheba, and Jacob at Bethel, were monuments to their observance of family worship.

Moses made distinct provision for the religious instruction of children by their parents. In Deut. 6: 6, 7, we read, "These words which I command thee this day shall be in thine heart; and thou shalt teach them diligently unto thy children (Hebrew—whet them diligently upon thy children, frequently repeating these things to them; as in whetting a knife, it is turned, first on this side, then on that), and shalt talk of them when thou sittest in thine house (resting thyself), and when thou walkest by the way (going to or from thy work), and when thou liest down (retiring at the close of the day), and when thou risest up, (to begin the work of another day)." First, let the word of God dwell in your own heart, and then seize upon every opportunity to impress that word upon the tender mind of your child. See also Deut. 4:9.

Look at the noble determination of Joshua in the presence of all Israel, as declared in our text, "As for me and my house we will serve the Lord." Neither his exalted station, nor his various and pressing public duties, prevented his attention to the religion of his family.

Call to mind the example of David. After he had brought the ark of God into Jerusalem, with gladness, sacrifices, and thanksgiving, and discharging all his public duties, and blessing the people in the name of the Lord, he returned to bless his household. (2 Sam. 6:20.)

When Zecheriah (12:12) predicts a great outpouring of God's Spirit he tells us " every family shall mourn apart."

And the Old Testament's closing words assure us of a time when "the hearts of the fathers shall turn to the children, and the hearts of the children to the fathers." Would you therefore live as godly men under the former dispensation lived, neglect not the worship of God in your family.

Coming to the New Testament we have equally clear examples in the observance of this holy duty. Our Lord's own example is emphatic. During his stay on earth, he stood as the head of a family, and his apostles were the members of his household (Matt. 10:25). How then did he act towards these members of his family? Did he not pray with them and for them, and was he not constantly instructing them? If, then you are a Christian you ought to walk even as he walked.

Cornelius is described as "a devout man, and one that feared God with all his house."

To the Phillipian jailor Paul said, " Believe on the Lord Jesus Christ and thou shalt be saved and thy house," intimating a close connection between the faith of the father and the salvation of his family.

The early Christians observed the worship of

God in their families. **Aquila and** Priscilla **had a church in their house.** (1 Cor. 16: 19).

Nymphas had **a church in his house,** (Col. 4:15).

Many were gathered **together praying in the house of Mary.** (Acts 12: 12).

And so in the after history of the Church. At the time **of the Reformation there was a** powerful **revival of family religion. Luther's "Table Talk"** **is still well worth** reading, **and his family prayers deeply impressed those who heard them. And need I remind you how our Scottish** forefathers highly prized the **worship of God in the** family? I have preached to **large congregations and** to small, in churches, in houses, in **barns, and under** the shade **of a tree, but** never have I felt more impressively the presence **of** God **than when I have** knelt with **a praying** family **on the earthen floor** of a little cabin in the Highlands of **Scotland.** There was **a time when in** Scotland **family** worship **was observed among the reapers in a barn. It was common on the fishing boats on the friths and lakes of Scotland. It was observed even in the depths of coal** pits. **What has given Scotland the** proud **position she occupies** to-day among **the nations of the earth? Is it her insular** position, **the wisdom of her** rulers, **the valour of her soldiers, or the** genius of her poets? **No, not at all. The secret of her** greatness **and her** prosperity **is to be** found **in the** Christianity among her **people. And this Christianity has been fed and nourished,** chiefly **at**

the family altar, amid such scenes as Robert Burns photographs in his "Cottar's Saturday Night."

> "From scenes like these old Scotia's grandeur springs
> That makes her loved at home, revered abroad.
> Princes and lords are but the breath of kings,
> An honest man's the noblest work of God."

This is the righteousness that has exalted that nation; and this righteousness more than the productions of our lakes, mines, fields and forests, will make this Dominion great and happy. The present degraded condition of the millions of heathen may be traced back to the neglect of the worship of God in the family. "Pour out thy fury" says Jeremiah (10: 25) "upon the heathen that know Thee not, and upon the family that call not upon Thy name."

II. Let me now indicate a few of the many benefits of family worship. And I will refer first, to the benefits to yourself as head of the family; second, the benefits to your family; and third, the benefits to posterity.

As to yourself, it will benefit you temporally. It promotes worldly prosperity. I will not dwell long upon this, for I would fain hope nobler motives will have more weight. Yet let it not be forgotten that true religion has the promise of the life that now is as well as of the life to come. Look at most families where the worship of God is neglected. What a want of order! What lack of authority on the part of parents, and of submission on the part of children! What jarring and

REV. W. A. McKAY, B. A., D. D.

Rev. Dr. McKay was born in Oxford County, Ont., March 11th, 1842. With seven years experience as a school teacher, he entered upon his academic studies in Toronto, and graduated from the University in 1869 and from Knox College in 1870. After eight years as a country pastor, he accepted a call to Chalmers Church, Woodstock, of which congregation he has been the faithful and honored minister for the past nineteen years. He stands in the foremost ranks of the temperance reform movement, and much valuable literature has emanated from his versatile pen, on this and other subjects. His famous work on "Baptism" has gone through fourteen editions, and should be read by any who have perplexities on that subject. In 1893 the Senate of the Presbyterian College, Montreal, conferred upon him the degree of D. D. in recognition of his theological scholarship.

dissensions! What alienation and premature breaking up of families!

But consider the spiritual advantages to yourself of uniting with your family in the fervent worship of God. Will it not serve as a check on you from wrong doing of every kind? When tempted to yield to anger, to speak hastily, or to act unkindly, your conscience will say, " Does this become one who is by and bye to kneel with his family at the altar, and pray against these very sins?" Many a one has experienced a nearness to God in family prayer that he does not always enjoy even in secret prayer.

But think of the benefits of family worship to your children. It diffuses sympathy between the members of the family. However simply conducted, it says to each member, " There is a God, there is a spiritual world, there is a life to come." It fixes the idea of responsibility in the mind of the child; and in a clear impressive voice says to each, " How shall we escape if we neglect the great salvation?" Children thus early instructed are far more likely to be good citizens for time, and hopeful candidates for eternity. The cloth that is dyed in the wool will keep the color best, and disciples in youth are likely to be steadfast in age.

And I would urge this duty upon you, not merely by the consideration of the good it will confer upon yourself, and those immediately concerned, but also by a consideration of the benefits to posterity for all time. Truth once started can never be wholly arrested.

> "The good begun by thee shall onward flow,
> In many a branching stream, and wider grow,
> The seed that in these few and fleeting hours,
> Thy hands unsparing and unwearied sow
> Shall deck thy grave with amaranthine flowers,
> And yield thee fruits divine in heaven's immortal bowers."

In Psalm 78: 4, 5, 6, the Psalmist speaks of five successive generations, and assures us that it is God's law that the fathers should each tell his children what he himself had learned from his parents, and thus transmit "the praises of the Lord" from generation to generation. Thus by honoring God in your family you are rearing for yourself a monument more enduring than brass, and that will last to all eternity to the glory of the grace of God in you.

Blessed is the dwelling place that is devoutly consecrated to the God of all the families of the earth. Whatever uncertainties hang to human view, over its future history; whatever changes it may witness; whether predominates there the voice of health and gladness or the wail of sorrow and pain; whether its larder be filled with plenty, or made lean by poverty; how oft soever its windows may be darkened by calamity and death—one thing is sure, it is the abiding place of the Most High; the angel of the covenant is there, and in the deepest night of grief, that home has light and hope and peace.

III. Finally let me mention two difficulties that

are frequently urged for the non-observance of family worship.

1. First, want of time. Well it is a busy age this, and I have no doubt but each one of you has enough to do. But what then? Surely this, that you who have so much to do, should all the more seek divine help and guidance. The more business, the more need of prayer, lest you become engrossed in the world and lose your soul.

But is it wise to give your time so exclusively to your earthly calling? Do you and your children not pay too dear for your wealth? Is the blessing of God a thing of so little value that you will not seek it only when you have nothing else to do?

And is it really true that you have no time, not even five or ten minutes to sing with your children, morning and evening, a few verses of a psalm or hymn, then to read a few verses of scripture and utter a word of prayer? In making this excuse are you really not deceiving yourself? Plenty of time to prepare food for the perishing bodies of your children, but no time to dispense the bread of life to their never-dying souls! I fear the real cause in most of cases, is not want of time, but coldness and indifference to the things of God, and to the eternal welfare of your family. Let these be removed and other difficulties will vanish like mists before the rising sun.

2. The other difficulty frequently urged is want of ability. This excuse is more popular than the

want of time, for it savors of humility; while pleading want of time savors of worldliness. But generally the one is as groundless as the other, the true reason being the want of will. How do you know that you have not ability to read and pray with your family? Have you tried? How often? You were not able to walk the first time you tried, nor to read, or write, but you can do these things now. You persevered, and though weak at first, exercise strengthened you. Can you not this very night, along with your family, read some verses, and then altogether repeat the Lord's prayer? That will be a good beginning. Try it. Resolve now with David (Ps. 132: 4, 5), "I will not give sleep to mine eyes, or slumber to mine eyelids, until I find out a place for the Lord, an habitation for the mighty God of Jacob."

I speak to you parents on this subject with great hopefulness, for I am pleading with you on behalf of your own children. You are not like the ostrich in the wilderness that careth not for her young. You are not of those who regard their children as "aliens from the commonwealth of Israel and strangers to the covenants of promise." As Presbyterians you do not think that your children must grow up in the wilderness of sin for many years, before they are brought into the garden of the Lord. Being yourself within the gospel fold it is your blessed privilege to regard your children as the "heritage of the Lord" (Ps. 127: 3), "born unto God" (Ezek. 16: 20), "the children of the covenant" (Acts 3:25), to whom pertain "the promise" (Acts 2:39). There has been no more solemn act of your life than when in the sacrament of baptism, you entered into a covenant with God on behalf of your child, promising that by the grace of God, you would bring up your child in the nurture and admonition of the Lord; and God on his part in infinite condescension entered into a covenant with you, promising to make His grace sufficient for you, and to bless you and your child, as you would be faithful to your engagement. How any one can thus covenant with God, and yet, with a quiet conscience, neglect the worship of God in their home I know not. Let me get admission to your heart while I plead with you. I know you are kind to your children, hospitable to your friends, attached to your minister, and loyal to your Queen, but are you forgetting God in your home? Alas that He who deserves more than any or all others, should be the only object of neglect. If this duty has been neglected in the past let it be so no more. Resolve at once that as for you and your house you will serve the Lord. So resolve, and this Sabbath will be a jubilee indeed to you, a day of gladness that you or yours will never forget.

Mothers, I admonish you. Much depends on you in this matter. I know a home where the worship of God was started by a mother, on a Sabbath evening, taking down the Bible, and gently saying, " Let us have worship to-night." Mothers, if necessary, go to-night and do likewise. And then when your boys are going to bed, be near them, smooth their pillow, give them a loving kiss, say God bless you; for the day will come when the weary couch will not receive either the kiss or the blessing.

Children, you too can do something in this matter. If you have given your heart to Christ walk humbly with God, and you may be the means of winning others in your home. The two daughters of a careless, irreligious father found Christ while away from home. The mother was dead. On the evening of their return home, they affectionately requested their father to establish family worship. He replied that he saw no use in it. He had lived fifty years without it, and he could not be burdened with it now. They then asked permission to pray with the family themselves. To this the father somewhat gruffly consented. Then one of the sisters took the Bible and read a chapter, they both kneeled, and the other engaged in prayer. And as the humble fervent prayer of that dear young Christian was ascending on devotion's wings to heaven, the father's knees began to tremble, his strong will yielded, and soon he, too, was on his knees, and then prostrate on the floor. Father and children wept together, and the Lord heard their cries, and that home was ever after a house of prayer to the living God.

The remonstrance of the child was effectual. And might not a similar suggestion, meekly and

MRS. REID.

MRS. NICOL.

MRS. GREGG.

The Survivors of the First Communion
in Nairn Church.

humbly made, by one of the children before me, be blessed of God? I have said enough. I leave the result to your conscience and God. May you be guided aright.

STRABANE.

BY REV. JAMES BLACK.

YE hills and woods of sweet Strabane,
    Your autumn beauties brightly shine
When sunbeams light up grove and plain
    And clothe with glory day's decline.

I stand upon a hill-top bright,
    The sun descends the western sky,
A scene of beauty meets my sight,
    A golden glory greets mine eye.

Beneath my feet lie fruitful vales,
    And spots adorned with lovely flowers,
As yet untouched by winter's gales,
    All beautified by sunny showers.

See, where yon orchard branches spread
    In beauty o'er the verdant soil,
While those, who underneath them tread
    Seize and enjoy the luscious spoil.

Behold those leaves of varied shade!
    The rainbow's colors all are seen;
How gayly are the woods arrayed
    In robes of yellow, red and green!

I see a cottage down below
    Where happiness has her abode,
Where shrubs, and vines, and fruit-trees grow,
    And hearts enjoy the peace of God.

Behold you place not far from here,
  At which arrives the daily mail,
With news of joy, the soul to cheer,
  Or tidings causing hearts to fail.

See yonder house of praise and prayer,
  Where young and old for worship meet;
May God Himself be present there,
  To bless them from His mercy seat.

Beside it see the place of tombs,
  Where precious dust, expectant, lies
Waiting the time when Jesus comes
  To bid its prostrate form arise.

Behold close by, the village school,
  Where teachers toil from morn to night,
To guide their flock by rod and rule—
  To train them for life's coming fight.

Not far beyond, among the trees,
  Peeps out the pastor's happy home,
The dwelling place of love and peace.
  To it may evil never come.

I dimly see sweet homes of love,
  As gentle twilight o'er them spreads;
May precious blessings from above,
  Be poured upon their inmates' heads.

May all thy children, sweet Strabane,
  Be taught the upward path to try,
Till, free from sin, and grief and pain,
  They sing the anthems of the sky!

OFFICE BEARERS, 1897.

SESSION.

Rev. D. G. Cameron, Moderator; Dr. James McQueen, Clerk; James Sanderson, **William Ferrier**, **George Nicol**, Alexander McFarlane and **Richard Lothian**.

BOARD OF MANAGEMENT.

William Dickson, Chairman; James **A. Gray**, Secretary; **John** Fulton, Treasurer.; Chas. A. Stewart; John Lothian and F. R. Balison.

BOARD OF TRUSTEES.

William Henderson, **Richard Lothian**, John Smith.

CHOIR.

Mrs. J. C. Williams, Choir Director; Miss Lothian, Organist.

SABBATH SCHOOL.

Rev. D. G. Cameron, Superintendent; William E. McFarlane, Secretary-Treasurer; F. R. Balison, Librarian; **Miss** McFarlane, Organist; Mrs. D. G. Cameron, Mrs. F. R. Balison, Mrs. John Lothian, Miss C. Fraser, Miss Janet I. Robertson, Miss E. F. Kee, Wm. Ferrier and the pastor, teachers.

W. F. M. S.

Mrs. D. G. Cameron, President; Mrs. P. Davidson, Hon. Vice-President; Mrs. R. Lothian and Mrs. C. A. Stewart, Vice-Presidents; Mrs. F. R. Balison, Secretary; Mrs. Wm. Dickson, Treasurer.

Y. P. S. C. E.

Wm. E. McFarlane, President; Miss E. F. Kee, Vice-President; Miss A. McNeill, Minute Secretary; Miss M. Brown, Corresponding Secretary; Miss A. Mitchell, Treasurer; Miss M. McFarlane, Organist.

"WHITE STONE" MISSION BAND.

Mrs. D. G. Cameron, President; Eppie Lothian, Vice-President; Minnie Warren, Secretary; Bertie Lothian, Treasurer.

Church Officer—Henry Barnett.

KILBRIDE—OFFICERS, 1897.

SESSION.

Rev. D. G. Cameron, Moderator; Alexander Fraser, Clerk; John Agnew, Edward Corlett and Isaac Clugston.

BOARD OF MANAGEMENT.

Edward Corlett, Chairman; Dr. G. B. Carbert, Secretary; John Turnbull, Treasurer; John Burns, Frank Small and Arthur Newell.

BOARD OF TRUSTEES.

A. Fraser, E. Corlett, J. Turnbull, J. Agnew and J. Burns.

SABBATH SCHOOL.

John Turnbull, Superintendent; John Agnew, Jr., Secretary-Treasurer; Cameron Turnbull, Mrs. J. Rutherford and Miss A. Cameron, teachers.

W. F. M. S.

Mrs. A. Fraser, President; Miss A. Cameron, Secretary; Mrs. A. Newell, Treasurer.

CONCLUSION.

When the foregoing pages came from the press, there were revealed a few minor errors, which had been overlooked in the correcting of the proof. On page 9, line 9, *further* should read *farther*; page 14, line 9, *June* should read *Jan.*; page 56, line 18, *this* should read *the*; and on the following line *subscriptions* should read *subscription*. Also at the top of page 58, it might have been stated, in addition to the other improvements, that unfermented wine was introduced at the communion, and at the bottom of page 65 might have been added the name of Mr. John Agnew, a pioneer of Nelson Township and a Kilbride elder of 39 years standing. Among our friends whose names appear in the list of offerings, are a number of professional and business men to whom we give space for advertisements and who are cordially commended to our readers.

Jubilee Offerings.

Abraham, Rev. Dr	Burlington, Ont	$1 00
Addison, Dr. James	St. George, Ont	5 00
Agnew, John	Kilbride, Ont	1 65
Amaron, Rev. Dr	Montreal, Que	1 00
Andrew, Archibald	Skead's Mills, Ont	1 00
Bain, Thomas. M. P	Dundas, Ont	5 00
Balison, F. R	Strabane, Ont	2 00
Balison, Mrs R	Roche Percee, Assa	1 00
Ballantyne, Rev. F	Kirkwall, Ont	1 00
Baxter A. B	Hamilton, Ont	1 00
Benham, W. W.	Cleveland, Ohio	1 00
Benham, Mrs. W. W	Cleveland, Ohio	1 00
Boyd, Mrs. John	Montreal, Que	2 00
Black, Rev. James	Hamilton, Ont	4 00
Black, Miss Jean B	Hamilton, Ont	1 00
Bronson, E. S.	Duluth, Min	1 00
Brown, Miss M	Freelton, Ont	1 00
Butler, A. E	Hamilton, Ont	3 00
Cameron, Miss Annie	Metcalfe, Ont	1 00
Cameron, Rev. D. G	Strabane, Ont	3 00
Cameron, Mrs. D. G	Strabane, Ont	3 00
Cameron, Geo. L	Strabane, Ont	1 00
Cameron, Lillian G	Strabane, Ont	1 00
Campbell, Rev. Dr. R.	Montreal, Que	2 00
Carbert, Dr. G. B	Kilbride, Ont	1 00
Carpenter, F. A	Hamilton, Ont	3 00
Cathcart, Rev. Dr	Cincinnati, Ohio	4 00
Chegwin, Mrs. Jas	Dundas, Ont	1 00
Connell, Richard	Valens, Ont	1 00
Corlett, Edward	Kilbride, Ont	1 65
Clugston, R. G	Kilbride, Ont	1 65
Davidson, P	Freelton, Ont	1 00

JUBILEE OFFERINGS.

Dickson, R. F.	Turin, Ont.	1 00
Dickson, William	Freelton, Ont.	1 00
Elliott, Thos.	Lowville, Ont.	1 00
Ferrier, Mrs. A. S.	Woodstock, Ont.	1 00
Ferrier, Dr. James	New York, N. Y.	1 00
Ferrier, Mrs. John, Sr.	Brandon, Man.	1 00
Ferrier, Wm.	Strabane, Ont.	1 65
Finch Bros.	Hamilton, Ont.	5 00
Flatt, J. I., M. P. P.	Hamilton, Ont.	5 00
Fletcher, Rev. Dr.	Hamilton, Ont.	4 00
Fraser, Alexander.	Kilbride, Ont.	1 00
Fraser, Miss C.	Strabane, Ont.	1 00
Fulton, John.	Freelton, Ont.	1 00
Galloway, Mrs. E.	Strabane, Ont.	1 00
Gilmour, Matthew.	Westover, Ont.	1 00
Gray, James A.	Freelton, Ont.	1 00
Gray, Henry.	Freelton, Ont.	1 00
Hall, Mrs. M.	Portage La Prairie, Man.	1 00
Hall, J.	Hamilton, Ont.	3 00
Harper, James, Sr.	Westover, Ont.	1 00
Harper, James, Jr.	West Flamboro, Ont.	1 00
Hazell, A. T.	Hamilton, Ont.	3 00
Henderson, William.	Strabane, Ont.	1 00
Johnstone, J. R.	Milton, Ont.	1 00
Johnstone, Miss M.	Strabane, Ont.	1 00
Kee, William.	Strabane, Ont.	1 00
Laybourn, Geo.	Kilbride, Ont.	1 15
Lennie, Mrs. Jas.	Guelph, Ont.	1 00
Lindsay, John.	Westover, Ont.	1 00
Lindsay, Mrs. J., Sr.	Westover, Ont.	1 00
Lindsay, Geo.	Westover, Ont.	1 00
Lothian, John.	Strabane, Ont.	1 00
Lothian, Richard.	Strabane, Ont.	1 65
Lothian, R. W.	Strabane, Ont.	1 00
McCuen, Miss Lizzie	Freelton, Ont.	1 00
McFarlane, Alex.	Strabane, Ont.	2 40
McFarlane, Miss Nellie	Victoria, B. C.	1 00

JUBILEE OFFERINGS. III

McHattie, Mrs. Thos	London, Ont	1 00
McIlroy, S. R	Hamilton, Ont	5 00
McKay, Rev. Dr	Woodstock, Ont	2 50
McLeod Mrs. D	Guelph, Ont	1 00
McNary, Mrs. D. L	Chicago, Ill	1 00
McQueen, Dr. James	Freelton, Ont	5 65
Mehaffey, Miss M	Freelton, Ont	1 00
Mills, Stanley	Hamilton, Ont	1 00
Minorgan, Mrs	Hamilton, Ont	1 00
Mitchell, Alex	Hamilton, Ont	5 00
Molineaux, James	Kilbride, Ont	1 00
Mylne, Mrs. A	Strabane, Ont	1 00
Newell, Arthur	Kilbride, Ont	1 00
Nicol, Geo	Westover, Ont	3 15
Nicol, John	Rothy Norman, Scotland	1 25
Nicol, John	Regina, Assa	1 00
Nicol, James	Shoal Lake, Man	1 00
Nicol, Miss Lizzie	Westover, Ont	1 00
Nicol Robert	Waimate, New Zealand	1 00
Peebles, Robert	Nelson, B. C	1 00
Reid, Hugh	Freelton, Ont	2 00
Robertson, Mrs. Chas	Strabane, Ont	1 00
Robertson, Rev. J. L	Gore Bay, Ont	4 00
Robertson, Mrs. Jas.L	Strabane, Ont	1 00
Robertson, J. R	Franklin, Pa	1 00
Robertson, Mrs. R	Freelton, Ont	1 00
Robertson, Rev. W	Morriston, Ont	1 00
Robertson, W. M	Warren, Pa	1 00
Rodgers, John	Strabane, Ont	1 00
Ronald, Wm	Westover, Ont	1 00
Ross, John R	Portage La Prairie, Man	2 00
Ross, Mrs. John	Freelton, Ont	1 00
Ross Miss Janet	Puslinch, Ont	1 00
Rutherford, James	Strabane, Ont	2 00
Rutherford, John	Strabane, Ont	1 00
Rutherford, John	Kilbride, Ont	1 00
Sanderson, James	Strabane, Ont	2 40

Sanderson, Hugh	Minnedosa, Man	1 00
Simpson, Mrs. W. H.	Hamilton, Ont	1 00
Simpson, R.	Guelph, Ont	1 00
Shanks, Dr. J. C.	Howick, Que	2 00
Shaw, Mrs. Thos	Montreal, Que	2 00
Sheridan, Mrs. R.	Freelton, Ont	1 00
Small, Frank	Kilbride, Ont	1 00
Small, George	Kilbride, Ont	1 00
Smith, Daniel	Freelton, Ont	1 00
Smith, John	Strabane, Ont	1 00
Stewart, Rev. John	Carlisle, Ont	1 00
Stewart, Alex.	Freelton, Ont	1 25
Stewart, C. A.	Strabane, Ont	1 00
Stewart, Peter	Strabane, Ont	1 00
Stewart, T. J	Hamilton, Ont	5 00
Tennant, Mrs. E.	Hamilton, Ont	1 00
Thomson, R.	Hamilton, Ont	1 00
Thompson, Dr. Chas	Hamilton, Ont	3 00
Turner, Mrs.	Tiffin, Ohio	1 00
Waddell, James	Foxwarren, Man	2 00
Wardrope, Rev. D.	Teeswater, Ont	1 00
Wardrope, J. W.	Little Cascapedia, Que	2 00
Wardrope, Rev. Dr.	Guelph, Ont	5 50
Wardrope, W. H.	Hamilton, Ont	3 00
Watt, George	Westover, Ont	1 00
Williams, J. C	Freelton, Ont	3 00
Williams, Mrs. J. C.	Freelton, Ont	1 00
Wilson, John	Hamilton, Ont	5 00
Wilson, Mrs. Thos	Freelton, Ont	1 00
Wyse, Mrs. B.	Puslinch, Ont	1 00
Young, Rev. John	Hamilton, Ont	3 00
Smaller sums		39 40

HARDWARE.

We are up-to-date in our business. Our Prices are right, our Goods are First-Class, and we have THE BEST HARDWARE STORE AND WAREHOUSE IN THE CITY. We carry full lines of

ROPE	OILS AND GLASS
CHAIN	FILES
BUILDERS' HARDWARE	BELTING
SAWS	WOOD SPLIT PULLEYS
AXES	MACHINE OILS
HARVEST TOOLS	PIPE IRON AND LEAD
PAINTS	PIPE FITTINGS.

We Solicit Your Trade in these lines and will give THE BEST OF ATTENTION.

F. A. CARPENTER & CO.,
77 AND 79 YORK STREET,
CALL IN AND INSPECT. . . . HAMILTON, ONT.

... Hazell & Son ...

DEALERS IN CHOICE

FAMILY GROCERIES

STORES:

Corner King and McNab Streets.
Corner Main and Wentworth Streets.

HAMILTON, ONT.

♥♥♥♥

GIVE THEM A TRIAL.

ISSUER OF MARRIAGE LICENSES.

J. C. WILLIAMS,

General ○ Merchant

FREELTON, ONT.

FURNITURE A SPECIALTY.

UNDERTAKING IN ALL ITS REQUIREMENTS

WHEN YOU WANT THIS PRESCRIPTION FILLED

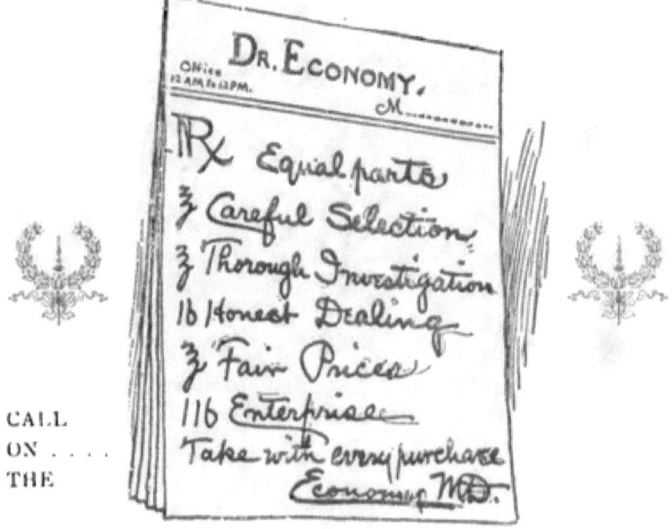

CALL ON .... THE

DUNDA'S DRUG COMPANY
E. SCARLETT.

ALEX. MITCHELL,

(FORMERLY OF WATERDOWN).

Chemist and Druggist,

GRADUATE OF THE ONTARIO COLLEGE OF PHARMACY, TORONTO,

HOLDER OF A DIPLOMA FOR ANALYTICAL CHEMISTRY.

GORE
DISPENSARY

Cor. York
and
Merrick
Sts.
Telephone
1255.

EAST END
PHARMACY

Cor. King
and
Ashley
Sts.
Telephone
977.

A FULL STOCK OF DRUGS,

Chemicals, Dye Stuffs, Drug Sundries, Toilet Soaps, Sponges, Perfumes, Paints, Oils, Brushes, Toilet Articles and Physicians' Supplies of all kinds, which are

 WARRANTED GENUINE AND OF THE VERY BEST THE MARKET CAN SUPPLY.

Physicians Prescriptions and Family Receipts carefully compounded.

· · · · **OBLIGING CLERKS** · · · ·

Every article guaranteed satisfactory or money refunded.

WHEN YOU REQUIRE ANYTHING IN THE DRUG LINE YOU WILL FIND IT BOTH A PLEASURE AND A PROFIT TO DO BUSINESS WITH US.

Hamilton Granite Works.

Corner York and Bay Streets.

T. J. STEWART, Proprietor,

WHOLESALE AND RETAIL MANUFACTURER
. . . OF

Monuments ∴ Headstones,

STATUARY,

BUILDING WORK, VAULTS, PLATFORMS, ETC.

Please do not place your orders until you have procured my prices which are of the lowest consistent with first-class stock and finish.

My manufacturing plant is equipped with all the modern conveniences for handling and working Granite.

Being a manufacturer and not merely a dealer means that buying direct from me you get your work at first cost, thereby saving to you the dealer's profit.

Visitors desiring to examine stock and compare prices will be courteously received and attended to.

T. J. STEWART.

Corner York and Bay Streets,
   Hamilton, Ont.

WE INVITE YOU HERE. . . . .

Finch Brothers.

**ONE OF THE FOREMOST
DRY GOODS STORES IN HAMILTON,
AND ONE OF THE
BEST KNOWN ♣ ♣ ♣ ♣ ♣
AND MOST POPULAR.**

WE send two buyers abroad every season and are large importers. We are constantly receiving new goods and styles from abroad, and this should be a good place to buy. We are always pleased to see our old friends and make new ones, and endeavor to have all purchases satisfactory. If goods are not as represented they can be returned and the money will be refunded at once.

We are Dress Makers, Mantle Makers and Milliners, and there is no house any place that can turn out a better class of work. We guarantee you lowest prices always. We invite you here.

**FINCH
BROTHERS,**   *Nos. 18 and 20
King Street West,
Hamilton*

Grafton & Co.

Manufacturers of Fine ♥♥♥♥

READY-TO-WEAR **Clothing**

At Manufacturers' Prices. ♥♥♥♥♥♥♥♥♥♥

ALL CLOTHING HAND-CUT, TAILOR-MADE, AND EQUAL IN EVERY RESPECT TO FIRST-CLASS CUSTOM WORK.

Factory and Warehouse:
King Street, Dundas.

Branches:
Hamilton, London, Owen Sound and Peterboro.

Happy Thought Range

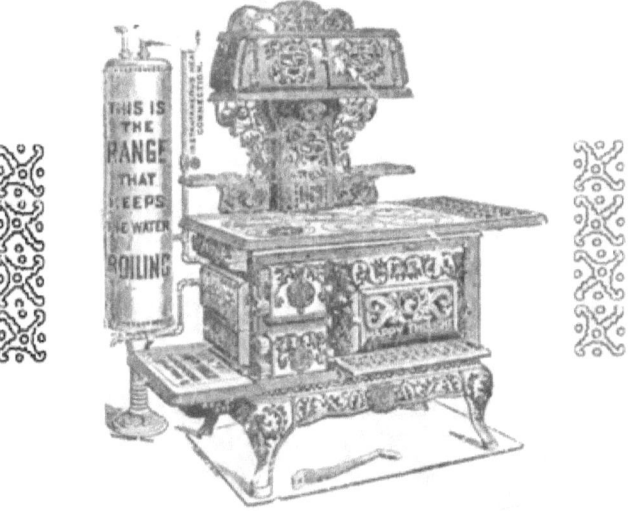

WHEN BUYING A RANGE BE SURE YOU GET THE GENUINE

BUCK'S HAPPY THOUGHT RANGE.

A full line of Stoves, Ranges and Tinware always on hand.

> REFERENCES
>
> CAN BE HAD FROM THE
> MANSE, IN STRABANE
> . . . OR FROM ANY OF THE
> **85,000 Families**
> IN CANADA NOW ENJOYING
> THE COMFORTS . . . .
> OF THE . . . .
> HAPPY THOUGHT RANGE.

Jobbing and . . . . Repairing Promptly Attended to.

JOHN WILSON,

7 AND 9 YORK ST.   **HAMILTON.**   8 AND 10 MARKET ST

W. H. Wardrope,

ARRISTER, SOLICITOR, ETC....

No. 34 MAIN STREET EAST,

HAMILTON.

DEEDS, WILLS, ETC. DRAWN.
MONEY TO LOAN.

Drs. Alton & Thompson,

DENTISTS,

No. 97½ King St. East

Opp. Ladies' College,

Office Hours:
9 a. m. to 6 p. m.

HAMILTON, ONT.

A. E. Butler & Co.

····Dealers In····

Ladies' and Gentlemen's Fine

BOOTS AND SHOES

RUBBERS, SLIPPERS, ETC.

Cor. James and Rebecca Sts.

HAMILTON, ONT.

Your patronage respectfully solicited.

1084
Safety...

There is no guess work in this store. There are no "IFS" and "ANDS" about a transaction with us. Our proposition is as simple as A. B. C. We propose to sell you safety in the shape of reliable FURNITURE. We are going to put the prices so low that no one else can go lower and keep out of the sheriff's hands. That's our proposition.

....COME AND GIVE US A VISIT.....

J. T. HALL,

37 AND 39 KING STREET WEST,

HAMILTON, ONT.

FRANK C. McILROY,

SPECIALIST ... IN

PRINTING, STATIONERY, BOOKS AND GAMES,

No. 89 King Street East, Hamilton.

PRESBYTERIAN BOOKS OF PRAISE, BIBLES, HYMN BOOKS.

N. B.—School Books and School Supplies a Specialty.
SEE US ANYHOW.

.... THE ....

MUTUAL RESERVE FUND LIFE ASSOCIATION

OF NEW YORK.

F. A. BURNHAM, ESQ. .. .. PRESIDENT.

Head (or Home) Office for Ontario .. Freehold Loan Building, Toronto.
W. J. McMurtry, Esq., Manager.

The largest, safest and best Life Insurance Company in the world.

Issues FREE and LIBERAL policies on acceptable lives from ages 18 to 60 years, at the lowest possible rates of premium consistent with absolute security and safety—containing the following and other special advantages:

    1st—Cash Surrender Value at any time after fifth year.

    2nd—Cash Dividends Annually, after eleventh year.

    3rd—Cash in a Lump Sum to the amount of one-half the "face" of the policy will be paid at any time after acceptance of policy in the event of Total Permanent Disability of the insured—from any cause, disease or accident, etc, to which all are more or less liable.

    4th—And No Restriction as to Travel, Occupation or Residence.

The majority of prudent people insure against FIRE that may never happen, yet are sometimes tardy if not careless about insuring against DEATH. That is absolutely certain to occur sooner or later.

References kindly permitted to Rev. D. G. Cameron, Strabane, and other eminent divines, professional and business men insured with us on application to ·

S. R. McILROY,

General Agent and Local Treasurer, Hamilton, Ont.
Office—89 King St. East.

The following letter will represent to the reader what practical Life Insurance really is.

S. R. McILROY, Gen'l Agent,
89 King Street East, Hamilton, Ont.

GUELPH, ONT., April 7th, 1893.

W. J. McMURTRY, ESQ.,
Manager Mutual Reserve Life Association,
Toronto, Ont.

Dear Sir,—Permit me to acknowledge, with thanks for your prompt and courteous attention, the receipt of check No. 6368 on Fourth National Bank, New York, for $20,000 in my favor as the executor of the last will of the late J. B. Armstrong, being payment in full claim, under Policy No. 45,962, held by him in the Mutual Reserve Fund Life Association of which you are the manager for Ontario.

When the principles of your Association and the mode of conducting business were first brought to the attention of Mr. Armstrong, I am aware that considerable influence was brought to bear upon him to prejudice him against the Association; but, in the exercise of his own judgment (and the result has shown the wisdom of his decision), he came to the conclusion that it was both safe and advantageous to take out a policy of even an unusually large amount, the highest at that time taken out in your Company by any person in Canada.

A few years ago similar influence was brought to bear on him, and still further illustrative of his cautiousness and judgment, he visited the head office and made all enquiries into the standing and operations of the Association, with the result that he was quite satisfied with them, applied to have his line with them increased by $10,000, which would have made the total amount $30,000, an application which had to be refused on the ground of his being, at that time, more than fifty years of age.

That confidence in your Association has not been misplaced is proved by the readiness with which the claim has been acknowledged, this being even in anticipation of the later date you could have fixed, and which was soon after you had made all the enquiry you considered necessary into the case, and had become satisfied that the payment fell within the regulations of the Association. I am, dear sir,

Yours truly,
ROBERT TORRANCE,
Sole Executor Estate J. B. Armstrong.

www.ingramcontent.com/pod-product-compliance
Lightning Source LLC
Chambersburg PA
CBHW030256170426
43202CB00009B/772